It is necessary that the reader is familiar with the biblical passages relating to some of my experiences, I have therefore reproduced them at the relative points.

The names of some people in the book have been changed to protect their privacy.

I would like to thank Emma Ashe for her invaluable help in editing the manuscript, Jason Miller for his collaboration with the artwork and Stephen Ashe for all of his technical advice in publishing it.

The events in the book are not in chronological order because I never kept a diary; therefore I have grouped the events by theme rather than by dates.

ISBN: 978-1-84753-374-6

http://www.stmichaelsblog.com

The Gospel

According to

Saint Michael

The Archangel

Prologue

It was Christmas 2006, in my dream I was at the swimming baths; the pool was covered in green slime just like a neglected pond. A young mother with two children came up to me and thanked me for the book saying that it had been most helpful to her.

Even though contact with Saint Michael began in 1980, during my pregnancy with my third son, I perceived no hint from him that he wanted me to record these encounters in a book. It was not until 1995, in the back pew of a dusky church, waiting, as an uninvited guest for a wedding ceremony to begin, that he informed me of his wishes. I was unable to fulfil my promise to write the book until 2002 when I returned to live in England, after my marital break-down. I had been too busy being the mother of a dysfunctional family to take time out to write.

I was born 4th May 1944; to her dying day, my mother refused to admit that she had been pregnant with me when she married my father on the 17th day of the previous September. She insisted that I was premature even though I weighed over 10 pounds at birth. Perhaps guilt was the reason why she was unable to love me.

My childhood memories are of domestic violence and deprivation. I still recall the shame of being forced to tell lies to the rent collector, “Me mam’s not in,” whilst out of the corner of my eye I watched her, hiding behind the door encouraging me to be convincing by miming what would happen to me if I were not. I witnessed my father deliberately setting fire to our only armchair for the insurance money; the 13 shillings and 4 pence when it subsequently arrived kept the wolves at bay for another few weeks. The sad thing is that my experience was no different from thousands of other unwanted children that were born at the end of the 2nd world war to reluctant parents plagued by self-imposed poverty.

The train arrived in the central station of Milan, Italy on the 4th May 1965 at 6am; it was my 21st birthday. I’d left home as soon as I could, to escape the violence and ended up working in London as an office clerk. I decided I wanted to see the world so accepted a job as au pair to a rich Italian family in Milan. I married my husband 1st January 1969, we have three children and compared to my mother’s situation, I persuaded myself that I was happy. The two younger boys became completely out of control in their teens; my husband had no control over them and he sabotaged any attempts I made of rectifying the situation. Having no authority over the boys what-so-ever and feeling alienated from my husband, I left him on Christmas Eve 1999 and returned to England. We divorced in June 2004

1

I didn't want to abort; I felt that I had no choice. My marriage wasn't the happiest in the land and I already had two children aged 5 and 4.

I entered the clinic with trepidations; in my heart of hearts I knew it was wrong. It was Sunday evening and the nurses started to prepare me for the procedure taking place the next morning at eight a.m. I didn't sleep at all that night and was grateful the next morning for the first injection, hoping that it would calm my pounding heart; it did not. I was put on a trolley and wheeled to the operating theatre, halfway there, I heard a newborn baby cry; at the same instant, the child moved in my womb. I was less than two months pregnant so it was highly unlikely to be a physical phenomenon.

I realized that I couldn't go through with it. I also realized that I had not chosen the best time to inform my gynaecologist. I was wheeled into the operating theatre and saw him talking with the theatre nurse and anaesthetist. They continued their conversation for a few minutes, ignoring my presence, then the anaesthetist came towards me holding the syringe filled with the drug that would put me to sleep; when I awoke it would be all over; it was now or never. My first instinct was to make a run for it then common sense set in as I imagined myself running through a labyrinth of corridors searching for the room that contained my knickers. "Could I speak to you in private?" was the hoarse whisper that came out of my mouth. Three perplexed faces turned to stare at me; two left the room and the third raising its bushy eyebrows asked, "Yes?" I managed to mutter to my gynaecologist that I didn't want to proceed with the abortion and after a stunned look of disbelief, he ordered me not to utter the dreaded word. In Italy in those days, abortions were illegal. He was risking his career and a possible jail sentence if it were known why I was there.

Two hours later I was sobbing hysterically in front of my mother and husband, not at all sure that I had made the right decision. That night my husband took me to the cinema, hoping that it would distract me from churning everything over and over in my mind. The film was Kramer v. Kramer and towards the end of the film I started to bleed. I went straight home to bed while my husband telephoned my long-suffering gynaecologist; he probably cursed the day that I had ever walked into his surgery. After his examination, he told me that I was having a miscarriage and would most likely lose the baby. He advised me to stay in bed with ice packs and under no circumstances was I to get up. After three days of listening to screams and fights between my two sons; I realised that my mother was unable to cope; she didn't know the language. I decided to get up even though I was bleeding profusely. Before doing so, I said aloud, "I don't know if You exist or not, but if You do, I promise not to do anything to induce a miscarriage; Thy will be done." It was my first real prayer. The bleeding stopped instantly; it was as if someone had turned off the tap. Seven months later my third son was born weighing nearly five kilos.

I have started my story with the abortion because I honestly believe that this was a spiritual crossroads in my life. With hindsight, I now know that it was, if you like, a spiritual test, which I passed only just, by the skin of my teeth. If I had gone through with the abortion, my life would have been dramatically different. The material aspects of my life would have been emphasised to the detriment of my spiritual development. I don't suppose that I would have been punished in the classical sense of the word, but proceeding with the abortion would have verified my immaturity to receive the teachings that have had such a profound influence on me. I would not have had all of the mystical experiences that have marked my spiritual evolvement. I would not have the absolute certainty that God really does exist. I would not have had answered the many questions that I have asked over the years, and I would certainly not be sharing these questions, answers and experiences that have enriched me and now I hope you. This is not an autobiography in the classic sense of the word; I won't bore you with details of my deprived childhood; instead, I know Saint Michael wants me to reveal the episodes of my life that have led to the disclosure of the karmic relationships between myself and members of my family and how they are rooted in past lives. Everything that I am committing to paper is absolutely true, even though it seems incredulous, even to me.

It is important at this point, to point out that there are two ways of assimilating knowledge; direct and indirect. Indirect knowledge is gained by reading about other people's experiences or watching events evolve around others. Direct knowledge is when it happens to you. Nothing can substitute personal experience; it is the most powerful way of knowing. For example, you can learn everything there is to know about an orange, from books or the internet, but to really know an orange; you must experience it by touching one, smelling it and tasting it. Words can never completely convey an experience; some of the experiences that I have had to endure seem hard, even cruel, but they were necessary in order to have a lasting impact on my life.

2

The next significant incident happened when the baby was about 11 months old. It was the middle of the night and he woke me with his cries; he'd soiled his nappy. I'd finished changing him and had him in my arms when I realised that I was going to pass out. "Not until I put the baby down," I ordered sternly. The symptoms receded and I replaced the baby in his cot. As soon as I straightened up, they returned. I made a desperate rush for the bed; a soft landing, but missed and fell to the ground hitting my head hard on the tiled floor. When I regained consciousness, I was in a pool of vomit and had a sore head for weeks after.

It was after that fall that I started to see things that didn't exist in this dimension and hear voices when nobody but myself was in the room. When I retired for the night; it was as if there was a coloured television in my forehead above my eyes. The scenes depicted weren't always pleasant. I remember that in the beginning, as soon as I closed my eyes, horrible distorted faces would appear from nowhere. They looked like decomposing bodies; zombies just risen from the grave as in films. I was terrified; then the face of an American Indian with beautiful plumes in his headdress would appear and they would disperse. I was frightened of the Indian as well, so I used to jump out of bed and go into the kitchen to smoke cigarettes and drink coffee to keep myself awake. It couldn't last and I eventually had a nervous breakdown. The doctor prescribed sleeping pills so that I could finally have a good night's sleep. The sleeping pills allowed me to go from wide-awake to fast asleep without passing through the alpha zone where this kind of phenomena occurs. After a few months on sleeping pills, I had built up my strength but was reluctant to continue to take them in case of addiction. I stopped taking them one night and immediately the faces returned followed by the American Indian. I went back to the pills but at last one night I plucked up enough courage to confront him. "Who are you?" I asked mentally. The scene changed and I saw him being born from me, "Are you my son?" I inquired. He nodded his assent. "How did you die?" I continued. The scene changed again and I saw him being beaten to death by two cowboys with the butt end of their rifles. "Why are you up there (heaven) and I'm down here?" I asked. "Because I have forgiven them," he answered telepathically. At that moment the scene changed again and I saw myself as an Indian squaw. I had just emerged from my tepee when four young braves laid the body of my dead son at my feet. In that instant, I re-lived all of the hatred and resentment, the loathing and bitterness that I had felt at that time towards the people responsible for his death. It was a very powerful experience. That wasn't all; I recognised the two cowboys. In this lifetime they are two of my immediate family. When we reincarnate, we may change the colour of our skin, our gender, our creed and our race but there is something that stays the same; the expression of our eyes. I recognised those cowboys by their eyes and in this existence two or three hundred years later, they are two of my three sons.

That in a nutshell is how Saint Michael introduced me to the divine law of love, which is played out throughout the ages. Love frees, hate binds you to the object of your negative emotions more surely than any superglue. Clever isn't it? The negative emotions present at the time of death are reprogrammed in our future lives to give us the opportunity to deal with them. Past life enemies become present day family. The relationship between a mother and her children is the strongest that exists. At that time, I needed this information because I was having trouble with David, my second son. From being very small it seemed that he delighted in challenging me; obeying his mother was not an option. This information helped me to understand our tumult relationship and therefore deal with the problem more objectively. I love all three of my sons but David has a special place in my heart because of all the karma that we have between us. This present life is at least the fourth time that I know of, that we are together. Looking back on these lives, I am now in a position to see clearly my mistakes and therefore to avoid falling into the same traps again. I hope in this life to end the cycle of emotional conflict, but at the present time it is still ongoing.

This was my introduction to reincarnation. I'd never considered it before and it took me some time to accept it. Even now, I can't accept that a human soul can retrograde into an animal as the Hindu religion teaches. Once an animal has evolved into a human being, even if they squander that opportunity and according to our sense of judgement deserve returning to being one, the grace of God and perhaps the law of evolution prevent it. A caterpillar can turn into a butterfly; a butterfly cannot turn back into a caterpillar.

Jesus taught reincarnation. Karma is just another word for the law of sowing and reaping that he spoke about. The word reincarnation did not exist in Jesus' time; it was not coined until relatively recently.

In Matthew 11:14 Jesus said explicitly that John the Baptist was the reincarnation of Elijah, (*And if you are willing to accept it, he is the Elijah who was to come)* which I interpret as meaning that the spirit present in the body of John the Baptist was the same spirit that had been present in the body of Elijah about 8 or 900 years earlier.

He confirmed it in Matthew 17:11-13. After witnessing the transfiguration of Jesus, when Elijah and Moses appeared and talked with Jesus, His disciples Peter, James and John seem to be saying to Jesus on their way down from the mountain, *O.K. after what we have just witnessed, we might believe that you are the Christ, but we've one more doubt. How come Elijah has not appeared yet as scripture predicts? (Malachi 4:5 See, I will send you the prophet Elijah before that great and dreadful day of the Lord comes.)* Jesus replied, "*to be sure, Elijah comes and will restore all things. But I tell you, Elijah has already come, and they did not recognise him, but have done to him everything they wished. In the same way the Son of Man is going to suffer at their hands.* Then the Bible says, *then the disciples understood that he was talking to them about John the Baptist.*

In Luke 9:18 it is obvious by the question that Jesus asked his disciples, (*who do the crowds say I am?)* That Jesus discussed reincarnation with His disciples; it is even more obvious by the reply given to Him by them. *"Some say John the Baptist; others say Elijah; and still others, that one of the prophets of long ago has come back to life.* It can be assumed by their answer that the crowds believed in reincarnation as well.

The disciples of Jesus believed in reincarnation. Why else would they have asked Jesus the question in John 9:2 about the man blind from birth, *Rabbi, who sinned, this man or his parents, that he was born blind?* The question only makes sense if they took into consideration a previous life of the blind man.

The doctrine of reincarnation was upheld widely among the early Christians; so much so that the emperor Justinian who was head of the eastern churches deemed it necessary to denounce it in 553a.d. He excommunicated Origen (185-254a.d.) who up to that time had been a highly esteemed father of the early church, because of his teachings on reincarnation. The church must have felt threatened by the doctrine of reincarnation; because reincarnation affirms that every individual is responsible for the redemption of his or her own soul. The church saw itself as an intermediary between God and man. The threat of excommunication, which meant eternal damnation in hell's fire, was enough to keep most people in line. Even so, the annals of history are filled with the names of brave men and women who defied the church and dared to think for themselves.

3

I have been taught that each physical body is the perfect medium to facilitate the evolvement of that particular soul. The soul is the fusion of the emotional body, the mental body and the spiritual body. At death, the soul leaves the physical body and levitates to the earth's astral plane, which is divided into seven regions. Every planet is a living organism and as such has a physical, astral and mental plane or "body". Just as water seeks its own level, so the amount of unconditional love present in the emotional body determines where the soul starts its spiritual journey.

The seven regions of the astral plane vary in density. The three denser (lower) planes are the equivalent of hell envisioned by most religions. There we face all of the negative actions we have bestowed on others and experience all the hurt and anguish that we have caused them. Time spent in each region depends on the lifestyle just ended, but it is very necessary as the lessons learnt will be invaluable in order to prevent the same pain being inflicted in future existences. Although we cannot consciously remember our experiences between lives, they are imprinted on our soul, which at a spiritual level influences our decisions. The spirit is the "managing director" of the other bodies. Its influence over them depends very much on the importance given to each individual body. The more pampered the physical body, the weaker the influence the spirit has on it.

The middle region is the equivalent to the purgatory of the Christian religion; in it indifference reigns. Souls stay in this region for a long time; in the physical body, they spent their lives doing neither good nor evil. In the Apocalypse they are accused of being neither one thing nor the other. *I know your deeds, that you are neither cold nor hot. I wish you were either one or the other! So, because you are lukewarm-neither hot nor cold-I am about to spit you out of my mouth.* (Revelation 3: 15-16) It is very difficult to escape from this region. Souls usually stay here for era after era, living an existence of apathy and monotony.

The three higher (less dense) regions are the equivalent of paradise contemplated by most religions. Here the soul basks in all of the love and kindness it has bestowed on others throughout its life on earth.

After completing the journey through all of the seven regions of the astral plane, the emotional body dies and the soul containing the mental and spiritual bodies proceeds to the mental plane. This too is divided into seven regions. Which plane the soul levitates to, depends on the amount of truth contained in the mental body.

In the three lower regions there are magnificent halls of learning. There, souls are brought face to face with any false dogmas, flawed reasoning, or misconstrued ideas that they held as part of a nation or of a community. This is done collectively and in general terms. The power of thought is explained and how it affects not only the individual but also their family, community and country. By the law of like attracts like, these thoughts congregate together and gathering momentum, form general karma making every person responsible for national decisions such as the war in Iraq. Negative thoughts become so powerful as to induce volcanic eruptions and tsunamis.

The middle region is where we examine our individual attitudes. We realise why we were attracted to a particular religion or political party or social group. Here we see unrolled before our eyes, all of our past lives and can see the reasons why it was necessary to endure those experiences in those specific circumstances in all of our different lives. The mental body gradually cleanses itself and with the help of gentle and kind beings undergoes a purging process.

The three higher regions of the mental plane contain all creativity and all knowledge of the past, present and future. Here, the mental body has access to the actual occurrences of historic events, which are not necessarily the biased accounts reported in the history books. Knowledge is communal in these regions and every mental body has access to it. This is where Mozart, Einstein and Leonardo da Vinci received the embryo of their creative ideas each in their own particular field. The mental body eventually dies and the spirit is left completely alone. It has been stripped of its personality, individuality, egoism and character and stands completely naked before God.

At this point, one of two possibilities occurs. Either the spirit realises that it has reached perfection, (Matthew 5:48 *"Be perfect therefore, as your heavenly father is perfect."*) and is ready to leave the cycle of incarnations and be reunited with the rest of humanity that has "made it" which will form the future body of God. Or it feels ashamed because naked it can see its own imperfections and realises that it needs further incarnations in order to eliminate them. It therefore starts its downward journey through all of the mental and astral planes attracting like a magnet everything it needs for its future incarnation. This is the real meaning of the fall of Adam and Eve. (Genesis chapter 3:1-21)*Now the serpent was more crafty than any of the wild animals the Lord God had made. He said to the woman, "Did God really say, 'you must not eat from any tree in the garden'?" The woman said to the serpent, "We may eat fruit from the trees in the garden, but God did say, 'You must not eat fruit from the tree that is in the middle of the garden and you must not touch it, or you will die'." "You will not surely die," the serpent said to the woman. "For God knows that when you eat of it your eyes will be opened, and you will be like God, knowing good and evil."*

When the woman saw that the fruit of the tree was good for food and pleasing to the eye, and also desirable for gaining wisdom, she took some and ate it. She also gave some to her husband, and he ate it. Then the eyes of both of them were opened, and they realised that they were naked; so they sewed fig leaves together and made coverings for themselves

Then the man and his wife heard the sound of the Lord God as he was walking in the garden in the cool of the day, and they hid from the Lord God among the trees of the garden. But the Lord God called to the man, 'Where are you?' He answered, 'I heard you in the garden, and I was afraid because I was naked; so I hid.' And he said, *'who told you that you were naked? Have you eaten from the tree from which I commanded you not to eat?' The man said, 'The woman you put here with me she gave me some of the fruit from the tree, and I ate it.' Then the Lord God said to the woman, 'what is this you have done?' The woman said, 'The serpent deceived me, and I ate.'*

So the Lord God said to the serpent, 'Because you have done this, Cursed are you above all the livestock and all the wild animals! You will crawl on your belly and you will eat dust all the days of your life. And I will put enmity between you and the woman and between your offspring and hers; he will crush your head and you will strike his heel.'

To the woman he said, 'I will greatly increase your pains in childbearing; with pain you will give birth to children. Your desire will be for your husband and he will rule over you.'

To Adam he said, 'Because you listened to your wife and ate from the tree about which I commanded you, "You must not eat of it," Cursed is the ground because of you; through painful toil you will eat of it all the days of your life. It will produce thorns and thistles for you and you will eat the plants of the field. By the sweat of your brow you will eat your food until you return to the ground, since from it you were taken; for dust you are and to dust you will return.'

Adam named his wife Eve, because she would become the mother of all the living. The Lord God made garments of skin for Adam and his wife and clothed them.

The so-called "fall" is the journey taken by every imperfect soul from the presence of God, down through the different regions of each plane collecting its future personality, character and life experiences (fig leaves.) The garments of skin in verse 21 that God made for Adam and Eve are our physical bodies.

4

Not every soul is able to make it to the astral plane. The souls of people who were trapped in sex, drugs, alcohol, or material possessions etc. at the time of their death become earthbound spirits. That means that they are so attached to the physical sensations of pleasure, that they literally cannot be separated from their compulsion. Matthew 6 verse 21 reads, *For where your treasure is, there your heart will be also.*

Saint Michael's teachings weren't always pleasant. Quite a few were definitely traumatic. One day bored with sewing, I decided to look for a video in my son's room. David had a lot of interesting music videos; I was looking for one by Bob Marley or the Doors. I picked up a few from his bedside table and went downstairs again. I inserted one in the video recorder and returned to my sewing. I glanced up at the television screen and froze. It was a pornographic film. I immediately switched it off and started to churn over in my mind what action to take towards my seventeen year old son.

That night my husband and I made love. Even though I had seen the film for only a few seconds, it had aroused me sexually. Later I awoke abruptly, I couldn't breathe; someone was using me for oral sex. As soon as I realized what was happening it stopped. I knew instinctively that it was an earthbound spirit, someone, that at the time of his death had been trapped by his sexual appetite. Everything emits vibrations; that deprived being had been able to attach itself to the video, because the vibrations of the video were in complete synchronicity with his own. The fact that I had watched the video even for a few seconds was enough to lower my vibrations and make me vulnerable to abuse.

I was furious, not only with that vile creature, but with Saint Michael, my guardian angel. I couldn't believe that he had not protected me. It wasn't that he couldn't protect me, but that he had chosen not to. Why?

The next day I was very irritable. At that time we had Mario staying with us. I considered him, and still do, my spiritual son. He was addicted to heroin and had been in trouble with the law. Instead of prison, he was on house arrest with us. He was very capricious but normally I had enough patience to deal with him; that day I did not.

As soon as he started his antics, I snapped at him; my troubles were bigger than his. I regretted it immediately but it was too late, he left and did not come home that night. The next day I was informed that he was in hospital; he had collapsed after taking heroin for the first time in months.

I continued my daily routine the best I could in the days following; I don't suppose anybody noticed that something was wrong. White spots appeared in my mouth and it was so painful that I couldn't bear my dentures in. I knew that it was crucial that I heightened my vibrations. This could be done by prayer and fasting. I had no difficulty in fasting, but I just could not bring myself to prayer. I tried and tried but just couldn't do it. I knew that Saint Michael had not abandoned me; it's just that I couldn't forgive him for allowing that loathsome creature to abuse me.

A few days later I was in the cemetery, (I was a florist) changing the flowers on one of the graves I tended. A complete stranger stepped out from behind one of the headstones nearby and started to recite a love poem to me; I couldn't help but smile. I knew that it was Saint Michael's way of trying to make up, but I still felt too hurt to respond positively. Later that afternoon, I was changing the water of a vase of roses when I noticed that one of the roses was taller and more beautiful than the others. I was silently admiring it when I heard Saint Michael saying, *that rose is you.*

We eventually became friends again and when I asked why it had happened he replied, *you asked why there was so much wickedness in the world. There is your reply. Just as a snowball rolled in fresh snow becomes very quickly a huge mass, so a small misdeed attracts to itself other misdemeanours and in no time at all becomes a huge transgression out of control.*

Mario could have died and indirectly I was to blame. At the same time I would never have seen that video if it had not been introduced into my house. Going further, nobody would have seen it if it had never been made, so whose fault was it? Everybody's and nobody's!

Carl Jung wrote that building a life was like building a house, the basic material, bricks are needed. The more bricks you have, the bigger the house you can build. The building bricks of a life are experiences; the more you have, even negative, especially negative, the bigger the life. The shocking, direct experience that I had just endured was to me equal to a ton of bricks. The lesson I learnt was to try to be correct even in the small things; especially in the small things, before they get out of hand.

I was careful what questions I asked Saint Michael after that and very careful not to go looking for videos ever again in my son's room.

****

Everything emits vibrations. I once bought a book written by a well known journalist about the life of a prominent member of the Italian mafia. After I had finished reading it, fore some reason or other it ended up in my car. Some time later while accompanying my children to school, the brakes didn't work and I very nearly had an accident. I immediately drove the car to the garage and left it there to be serviced. I cleared it of all my personal stuff, including the book before I left. The next day the mechanic phoned me and said that there was nothing wrong with the brakes.

After that experience, I'm always very careful about what books and DVD's I allow into my house. Prohibited subjects for me are anything on ghosts, poltergeists, witches, voodoo, serial killers or any other violent or negative material, even violence in comics I do not allow.

5

I've always had difficulty in trying to imagine God. Jesus portrayed Him as a loving father but I couldn't identify with that, probably because my earthly father was anything but loving.

One day after picking the boys up from nursery school, I asked them what sort of day they had had and David started to tell me the story that his teacher had told him. As it unfolded I realised it was the answer to the question I had asked myself for years; who or what is God?

Once upon a time there lived two brothers in the ocean, Little Drop was the name of the younger, Big Drop that of the elder. One day they were separated and Little Drop searched desperately for his elder sibling. "Big Drop where are you?" he called, swimming frantically all around the ocean. A wise old fish heard him and advised him to look higher up. Little Drop swam higher and higher until he was floating on the surface of the water. He suddenly felt light-headed and soon realised that he was suspended in the air above the ocean. The heat of the sun had turned him into vapour and together with lots of his friends, he found himself being drawn higher and higher into the sky. He started to shiver; a cold wind was blowing them inland towards the mountains. Suddenly without warning, he found himself falling; he and his friends had been turned into snowdrops and they were all very afraid. He heard someone calling his name and turning around; to his joy saw that it was his brother. They both landed together softly on a ridge high up on the northern side of a mountain and remained there all winter. When spring came they started to melt and together with their friends became a trickle of water, which flowed down the mountain into a waterfall, which fed a lake, which flowed into a river, which finally returned them to the ocean from whence they had come in the first place.

That night I asked Saint Michael what the story meant. This is what he said. *As you have difficulty in imagining God as a loving father, think of him as an ocean. When you analyse a drop of water you find H2O, two molecules of hydrogen to every molecule of oxygen. If you were to analyse God, you would find L2T, two molecules of love to every molecule of truth. In the bible it says that God is love, which is true but it is not complete, God is also truth. If God were only love, there would be no justice because love is all forgiving. If God were only truth there would be no mercy because truth is unforgiving. Together they are perfect; they modify each other; God is absolute love and absolute truth.*

You are Little Drop; you are love and truth in relative. When your life on this earth is ended, all of the love you have accumulated in your heart, together with all of the truth you have accumulated in your mind will leave your physical body and return to God, from whence you came in the beginning.

That story helped me a lot to piece together bits of the jigsaw. I concluded that it doesn't matter if we are Christians, Moslems, Jews, Buddhists, Sikhs, Hindus, atheists or whatever else people define themselves as, what is important is how much love and truth we have accumulated during our life before death.

The second consideration is, if God is love and truth, how can atheists really exist? How can anybody refuse to admit that love exists or that truth is not a reality? Atheists can only exist if they contest the existence of a human-like God who points his finger at the least demeanour, or of a Santa Claus type God who concedes all to his spoilt-brat children, and then I suppose most of us are atheists. The verses of Saint Paul come to mind, *When I was a child I talked like a child, I thought like a child, I reasoned like a child. When I became a man, I put childish ways behind me (1 Corinthians chapter 13 verse 11.)*

After hearing that explanation from Saint Michael, I can honestly say that I feel that I have finally come of age.

6

Praying has always been a chore rather than a delight to me; I couldn't see the point in it. One day, my eldest son aged eight was preparing for his first communion and had just received his book of catechism. On the front cover was a picture of Jesus with the words *I am always with you.* "That's a lie," objected David, his younger brother, "It's impossible that He's with you and everybody else at the same time." "It's not a lie," parried Patrick, "It's true." "How does it work then?" asked David challengingly. There was a moment of silence whilst Patrick searched for a rational response. "Like Multiman!" he said at last triumphantly. (Multiman was a cartoon character, who was able to save the world from devastating situations by transforming himself into thousands of replicas of himself; each one of them performing different tasks simultaneously in different places.) There is no (polite) English equivalent that I can think of, to portray the expression of complete disgust and incredulity on David's face, not to mention what came out of his mouth. Hurt to the core, Patrick realised that his theory needed to be sustained and approved by an independent and authoritative source. "Mamma?" Four eyes turned to scrutinise the ever wise, all-knowing, truth-defining sage sitting at the table with them. I writhed uncomfortably in my chair, biding for time, hoping for any distraction that would prevent me from uttering the words every parent dreads, "I don't know."

I prayed silently for help and to my surprise found myself saying and doing things that definitely did not originate in me. *Come with me*, I said and led them into the bedroom. I unplugged the lamp from the wall socket and unscrewed the bulb. I showed it to them and asked them what it was. "A bulb" they replied. *What does it do,* I continued. "It lights up the room," said David. *Why isn't it illuminating the room now then?* I asked. "Because it isn't plugged in," said Patrick impatiently and taking the bulb from me he screwed it into the lamp and plugged the lamp into the wall socket. It still didn't work until he had pulled the switch on the lamp. *What's in the wall that is so important to the bulb?* I asked. "Wires," they both said in unison. We followed the wires (it was an old house with external wiring) out to the hall out of the door onto the landing then down into the cellar. "Where do they go from here?" asked Patrick. *Under the pavement, uniting with all of the other wires from all of the other houses until they eventually arrive at the power station*, I replied.

We returned upstairs to our apartment and leading the way into the bedroom I once again unplugged the lamp from the wall socket and unscrewed the bulb. *Each one of us functions like this bulb,* I found myself explaining holding it up, *absolutely useless until we are connected with the power station (God) by the wires of prayer. Jesus is the electricity that comes from God along the wires and illuminates the bulbs. Not just one bulb but as many bulbs that want to be illuminated, but you have to switch on. Jesus, just like the electricity doesn't come uninvited. Some people prefer to sit in the dark rather than turn on the light. Jesus is with every person who desires his companionship by prayer, in the same way that millions of light bulbs are switched on every day in different countries at the same time.*

My attitude towards prayer changed from that day on.

****

Prayer is power. One night, returning from a prayer meeting, I ignored a give way sign; I didn't see it. Unfortunately two motor bikes were coming along at a tremendous speed; one managed to avoid me but the other one hit me full on. Both bike and rider were catapulted over the bonnet of my van hitting the hard tarmac at different angles. I screamed to Saint Michael to save the driver. Over and over I implored Saint Michael to save him. After what seemed an eternity, the man picked himself up, brushed himself down, picked up his bike and drove off with his companion without even giving me a glance. There was not a scratch on him or his bike.

Again in my car I experienced the power of prayer. I'd accompanied my son to Newcastle airport and on the way back the weather changed abruptly and in no time at all, the rain that had fallen on the roads that morning turned to ice. As I approached the corner where I should have turned left, up a hill to join the A68, I was dismayed to see cars and vans sliding down it or being pushed up it by their passengers. I should have stopped but if I had touched the brakes the car would have started to skid; if I didn't, I'd crash into the car just in front of me. I squeezed the brakes as gently as I could and as the car swung out of control I desperately started praying, indeed imploring Saint Michael to come to my rescue. He did. I somehow succeeded in turning the corner, whilst in a spin, without actually hurtling into anything. I still had to abandon the car further along the A68 but within a ten minute walk from where I live, not in the middle of nowhere.

At the beginning, like many others, I didn't know how to pray. Some people advised me that the quantity was of no importance as long as the quality was good. Others, that spontaneous prayer was better than the rosary or litanies of the Catholic Church.

Saint Michael came to my rescue. He led me to the Hebrew daily prayers which are anything but spontaneous. He still asked me to retain the rosaries and litanies that I used to dedicate to God, Jesus, the Holy Spirit, Mary and all the archangels. Indeed, he added another rosary asking me to dedicate it to Saint Joseph. I obeyed half heartedly because Saint Joseph as all of the saints of the Catholic Church had never been on my list of priorities. One day though, I needed divine intervention for one of my sons and I started praying to Saint Joseph fervently. His voice came through loud and clear, *that's more like it.* Since then we've been the best of friends. All in all, I suppose it takes me about three hours to complete my daily prayers.

On a pilgrimage to The Holy Land a few years ago, I was asked by the priest to choose what to dedicate our rosary prayers to. I thought about it for a while and then decided to dedicate them to all of the defunct members of our families. That night, in a dream, I saw every member of my family and my husband's family that had passed away. They were all posing in a semi-circle, as if they were having their photo taken. My aunt had my sister's baby in her arms and my father-in-law was in striped pyjamas lying in what looked like a hospital bed in front of them all. I asked him how he was and he replied, *much better. I've been very ill but I'm much better now.*

****

My son Patrick, aged sixteen had a dream that obviously troubled him because he came to me and asked me what it meant. I was at a loss for words as well and after a whole day of churning the dream over in my mind, I finally sat down and started to recite my rosary. While I was reciting my rosary, the whole meaning of the dream was explained to me in every detail.

This is the dream. Patrick was walking down the street when a taxi came along side of him. In the taxi were two brothers, friends of his father and at their feet was a dying man. They asked him if he was going their way and he accepted a lift from them to the railway station. Whilst waiting for the train, he suddenly espied his own two brothers walking towards him. They were walking on either side of a third person and were in animated conversation with each other. Patrick panicked and made a desperate attempt to avoid them by running away. His movement was hindered by a bucket full of heavy stones, which he was carrying. He awoke in a cold sweat.

This is the meaning that was explained to me. It was a warning to Patrick from his guardian angel because he was going down the same path as the two brothers in the taxi who hated one another. Their brotherly love was dying at their feet. The person walking between his own two brothers, represented the brotherly love that they felt for each other; very much alive. The bucket of stones was all of the resentment and animosity that he felt towards them.

That dream did help Patrick to face up to his negative feeling towards his brothers and resolve some of the issues he had with them.

****

Saint Michael told me the best time to pray. God has assigned each day to a different archangel. The day starts at about 6.00pm the previous evening, because according to the Genesis, *And there was evening, and there was morning (Genesis 1 v5-31).* Obviously God works to a lunar schedule instead of a solar one otherwise He would have said it the other way round, morning and evening.

These are the names of the archangels:

- The archangel Saint Tsafkiel who rules Saturn dominates from 6.00pm Friday night up to 6.00pm Saturday night.
- The archangel Saint Raphael who rules the sun dominates from 6.00pm Saturday night up to 6.00pm Sunday night.

- The archangel Saint Raziel who rules the moon dominates from 6.00pm Sunday night up to 6.00pm Monday night.
- The archangel Saint Michael who rules Mars dominates from 6.00pm Monday night up to 6.00pm Tuesday night.
- The archangel Saint Tsadkiel who rules Mercury dominates from 6.00pm Tuesday night up to 6.00pmWednesday night.
- The archangel Saint Kamiel who rules Jupiter dominates from 6.00pm Wednesday night up to 6.00pm Thursday night.
- The archangel Saint Gabriel who rules Venus dominates from 6.00pm Thursday night up to 6.00pm Friday night.

This concept is better illustrated with a coloured diagram rather than words. It is on the website **www. stmichaelsblog.com.**

During the twenty-four hours, the four best times for praying are from 6.00pm to 7.00pm, 1.00am to 2.00am, 8.00am to 9.00am, 3.00pm to 4.00pm, solar-time.

Each archangel has a different ministry; Saint Tsafkiel is the minister of intellect or understanding, Saint Raphael of healing, Saint Raziel of "Sapienza," (which I interpret as a merging of knowledge and intuition, knowing with your heart rather than with your mind.) Saint Michael of wisdom, Saint Tsadkiel of mercy, Saint Kamiel of justice and Saint Gabriel of compassion. So if for example, I pray to God for mercy, I make my petition on Tuesday night from 6.00pm to 7.00pm, or Wednesday morning between 8.00 and 9.00am or Wednesday afternoon between 3.00 and 4.00pm.

7

The human body is in continuous evolution. We are not just the physical body we can see and touch; we are much more than that. Surrounding our physical body is our etheric or mental body and surrounding that is our astral or emotional body. These bodies are usually referred to as our aura.

To develop, each body needs food. If we examine today's children, we find that in general, they are taller and healthier than the children of my generation or that of my mothers'. Indeed, in western countries so much food is available for their physical bodies that many children run the risk of becoming obese.

The mental bodies of today's children have evolved also. In 1905, when Albert Einstein made public his theory on relativity, there were probably only five or six people in the whole world that could appreciate it. Today, any bright college student is able to understand it. That means, from one generation to another, the human brain is evolving. Again, if when I went to school I was able to understand a concept at the age of ten; today, that same concept can be explained to seven or eight year olds and they have no trouble in understanding it.

The physical and mental bodies of humanity are evolving happily together thanks to the variety and amount of healthy foods available to them both. Bangers and mash nourish the physical; school programmes and the Internet nourish the mind.

The same has not happened to our emotional bodies. The negative emotions of fear, hate, resentment and envy are just as present in the generations of today as they were in my generation or that of my mothers and have been present in human society since the beginning of time. Why? Why is it that western society has been so successful in nurturing the physical and mental bodies of their peoples, but has failed miserably in nurturing their emotional bodies? Might it be because the well being of their emotional bodies has been delegated to organised religion? Our physical and mental bodies are well fed but our emotional bodies are starving for a lack of love, unconditional love. Parents have the bulk of the responsibility of teaching their children to be loving individuals by loving them unconditionally but even those of us who have a good relationship with our parents are still starving. What we do not receive, we cannot pass on to our children therefore the problem is perpetuated throughout the generations.

Every single adult is responsible for his or her emotional evolution and the emotional evolution of their children. Our physical, emotional and mental bodies should evolve together. If one is left behind, it's as if we are walking lop-sided. The same amount of food should be given to the emotional body as is given to the other two. Emotional food is love, unconditional love. We feed our emotional bodies by showing love, mercy, kindness, consideration, respect, tolerance, and compassion to others. No loving gesture goes unnoticed; it is imprinted on our soul even if the recipient does not appreciate it; eventually every loving thought, word and deed showered on others returns to enrich us.

8

I have always been fascinated with the stories in the Old Testament, especially the stories about the patriarchs. As a child my eyes were glued to the pages of my bible whilst reading about Abraham, Isaac and Jacob. I now know that was because I am the reincarnation of Jacob. All of my problems in this life stem from the mistakes I made in that one (Genesis 25:19 onwards.)

As Jacob, I was not a just man; I favoured one of my wives over the other one and I favoured Joseph, one of my sons over the other eleven; thus creating jealousy. I am still reaping that bitter harvest today in my present life. The law of karma, or if you prefer it, the law of sowing and reaping as Jesus taught, seldom occurs in the same lifetime. In my case, all of the jealousy and more that I created as Jacob, (renamed Israel by God) (*Genesis 37:3 Israel loved Joseph more than any of his other sons)*, came back to haunt me in my next life as Saul, the first king of Israel. (1 Samuel chapter 9 onwards.) Joseph, the son whom I had so favoured out of all proportion in my first life as Jacob, reincarnated as David at that time. When I as Saul heard the women singing, *"Saul has slain his thousands, and David his tens of thousands,"* (1 Samuel 18:7) all of the jealousy I had created in my other eleven sons in my life as Jacob, came back to me and it was so powerful that it sent me literally mad. It is indeed poetic justice when it is realised that the object of my jealousy as Saul, was in fact the object of my favour in my first life as Jacob.

I was not aware of these facts when my second son was born, how appropriate that I called him David.

I abandoned my family in Italy on Christmas Eve 1999 and came back to the UK to live. My youngest son was 19 at the time but I still have qualms of conscious every now and again because it was round about that time that he started taking heroin. He assures me that my leaving had nothing to do with it but I have my doubts. My life in Italy had become unbearable; David had turned my home into a squat. I can't even begin to convey the extent of the anguish I felt when my clothes went missing and later I'd see his girlfriend wearing them, the irritation when I could find no pans in the house to cook a meal with, because he frequently cooked for his fellow punks and didn't bring the pans back. The fright of waking up and finding six or seven Rasta individuals using my sitting room as a doss-house, each with their dogs growling at me when I came out of the bedroom. Being besieged by the neighbours with complaints about loud music, fights and arguments became intolerable. The sheer frustration of losing the daily battle of trying to keep clean a home that was in fact a squat was debilitating. When I complained to my husband, his reaction was, "He's young; he'll grow out of it." He was 23 and there was no sign of him changing course. I eventually gave my husband an ultimatum, either David left or I would leave him; I left.

In my life as Saul, I was responsible for David's exile. In this life, David with his behaviour is responsible for mine.

I have two options. I can either feel resentment therefore perpetuating this karmic drama into my next life, or I can forgive him and in so doing terminate this ongoing saga once and for all. I choose the latter but whether I will be successful or not remains to be seen.

<u>A chart to facilitate the complicated relationships between myself and others throughout my different lives.</u>

This lifetime	First Life	Second Life	Third Life	Fourth Life
Myself	Jacob	Saul	Mary Magdalene	Indian Squaw
My mother	Isaac (My father)	Bathsheba	-	-
My father	-	Uraiah	-	-
My brother	Esau (My twin brother)	-	-	-
My sister-in-law	Rebekah (My mother)	-	-	-
My husband	Ruben (My 1st son)	-	-	-
Patrick (My 1st son)	Zebulun (My 5th son)	-	-	Cowboy?
David (My 2nd son)	Joseph (My favourite son)	David King of Israel	-	Cowboy
Bengy (My 3rd son)	Benjamin (My youngest son)	Asaph (musical director)		Cowboy?
Mario (My spiritual son)	Issachar (My 6th son)	Jonathan (my son)	John the Apostle	-

9

I was busy preparing the evening meal when there was a knock on the door. It was two Jehovah's witnesses. I didn't want to be rude but was busy and didn't want to waste time. I compromised; I didn't invite them in, I hoped that by keeping them at the door my ordeal would be short and painless. The elder of the two started to read from the bible; they were trying to convince me that Mary had had other children after Jesus. I did not argue with them but my thoughts followed their own course. "It's not fair," I mused; "I know for certain in my heart of hearts that what these people are saying is not true, yet they have numerous verses in the bible that seem to corroborate their opinions. On the other hand, I cannot find one single verse to sustain my conviction, that Jesus was an only child."

I heard Saint Michael's voice in my head. *St. John's gospel, Jesus on the cross looked at Mary, his mother and said, "Woman, here is your son," He then said to John his disciple, "Here is your mother." From that day forth, this disciple took her into his home.* (John19:26-27.) *Close your eyes and imagine that you are there with them. Jewish law is very severe even today, do you really believe that it would have permitted Mary to go and live with a complete stranger if she had had other children alive, able to look after her? And again, do you really believe that if she had had other children that they would have allowed their mother to be cared for by a complete stranger instead of by them? And again, do you think that Mary would have preferred to be cared for by a stranger rather than by her own flesh and blood?*

I was delighted, so there was evidence in the bible to validate my beliefs after all.

This is Mary's story, as I understand it. When Saint Anne, Mary's mother realised that she was pregnant, she was overjoyed. Up to that moment everybody, including herself had thought that she was barren. After Mary's birth, Saint Anne's health went downhill and her husband who was a lot older than his wife, realised that there was a good chance that neither of them would live long enough to see Mary grow into adulthood. He decided to enrol her at an early age in a boarding school run by the priests at the temple. Saint Goachim was a wealthy merchant and he provided for Mary's future in the event of his death. Mary lived and was educated at the temple going home only to visit. That way her life was not too disrupted when the inevitable occurred; her parent's death. When her education came to an end between the ages of 14 and 15, Mary, like the rest of the young ladies should have been sent home to her parents but Mary was an orphan; she had nowhere to go. The priests decided that she should be married off and looked around for a suitable contender.

Saint Joseph was a widower; his wife had died a few years before. He was very religious and was esteemed as a respectable member of the community by the priests. They suggested to him that he should take Mary as his wife and he refused point blank; there was no way that he was going to take on a 15 year old girl. The Archangel Gabriel appeared to him in a dream asking him to reconsider his decision, as he had been chosen by God to protect her. The rest of the story is written in Matthew 1: 18-24.

Many people cannot accept the fact that the relationship between Mary and Joseph was not sexual. It was an arranged marriage; it was the normal procedure in those days. Love and courtship did not enter into the equation. Their relationship had been more of headmaster/pupil rather than that of a courting couple of today.

10

Things that happened to me after the birth of my third son in 1980, changed my attitude towards God, I now was beginning to believe that He existed, but I was still very hostile towards organised religion until I had this dream.

A man went to a jeweller's shop and showing a beautiful jewel to the proprietor asked him to create a suitable setting for it, as he wanted to bequeath it to his heirs. The jeweller inspected the jewel and was blinded by its beauty. He felt inadequate and so invited his illustrious colleagues to help him with the task. They all argued and debated, wrangled and compromised but eventually they created what to them was an appropriate setting for the jewel.

In due course the man returned to collect his jewel and was curious to see it in its new setting. He was appalled. It was covered so much in gold and silver and other precious and semi precious stones that the original beauty of the stone, its simplicity, was veiled; even he had difficulty in recognising it. He became very angry and looking up at the jeweller was about to chastise him, when he saw in the jeweller's eyes all of the inadequacy and incompetence felt by him. He limited himself to saying, "Thank you, I realise that you have done your very best and that is the most that I can ever ask of you. I'll take it as it is."

I asked Saint Michael what the dream meant. *Jesus is the man,* he said, *Christianity is the jewel, popes, bishops and theologians down the centuries are the jewellers, but if it's good enough for Jesus who are you to refuse it?*

The very next day I made arrangements at my local church to take religious instructions and at the grand old age of 38 took Holy Communion for the first time. Curiously enough, chance had it that I received it on Saint Benjamin's day the 31st March. For me, that was a sign from God that He had forgiven me for contemplating aborting my baby.

I didn't choose my baby's name, I didn't really like the name Benjamin; I was asked by Saint Michael to call him that. I compromised and named him Benjamin Giovanni Lorenzo. Giovanni is a family name and Lorenzo is the name I would have chosen for him; we call him Bengy

11

My husband insisted that our two older boys, aged four and five, learn to swim, so I took them to the swimming baths for lessons. From the very first lesson David's bathrobe went missing. He was upset because it had Goldrake printed on the back of it. Goldrake was their favourite cartoon character at the time and the identical bathrobes had been bought especially for the occasion. "I'm sure it's been taken by mistake," I comforted him; "It'll turn up next week." It didn't. We never saw it again until the end of the very last lesson when David came running towards me waving his robe triumphantly. "Look, at last I've found it," He exclaimed happily. An irate mother was following him "Give me back my daughter's robe," she said angrily. "It's not your daughter's," I said, "It's my son's; Look my other son has one exactly the same." She ignored me completely and wrenching it from my son's hands, stalked off. David immediately started to howl. "OK calm down" I said, "Just let's think about our options." I needed time to think, nothing so blatant had ever happened to me before. "We could go and fight her for it, but we aren't a violent family are we?" They both assured me that yes we were a violent family and that we should fight tooth and nail to get it back. I ignored them and went on to say, "Or, we could report her to the police but then she'd be put in prison and her poor daughters would starve to death and we don't want that do we?" They both nodded emphatically, relishing the prospect of a slow and painful death for her two repugnant offspring. "Or, we could turn the other cheek; after all we are trying to be good Christians aren't we? They weren't at all impressed with that suggestion but with bribes of ice cream and sweets I somehow managed to calm them down, dry them, dress them and get them home.

That night, I could hardly wait for my session with Saint Michael. "I hope you saw what a good Christian I was this morning," I said smugly. *You acted with wisdom,* was the reply. *As a wise Hindu, a wise Jew, a wise atheist but not as a Christian, because it is written that whosoever steals your coat, give him also your cloak.* (Matthew 5:40.) I was gob smacked! As a Christian, was I really expected to run after her and hand over my other son's bathrobe?

It was after this experience that I asked Saint Michael if he could suggest an historical figure that I could model myself on. His reply was, *Mahatma Gandhi*. "But he was not a Christian," I objected, "He was a Hindu." *Up here* (touching his forehead) *he was a Hindu,* Saint Michael replied, *but here* (rubbing his thumb and fingers together) *he was more Christian than any Christian.*

Years later, in England, I very foolishly shared this experience with an evangelical, born again Christian group. They immediately accused me of being possessed by demons and insisted on praying over me in tongues to drive them out.

What was it about Gandhi that was so appealing to Saint Michael more than any Christian saint? The first thing that struck me was the fact that Gandhi certainly didn't pamper his physical body. This probably cleared his life of a whole lot of unnecessary details that allowed him the time and space to dedicate to his passion in life, the seeking of truth. If God is truth, then indeed the path that Gandhi chose to seek Him is worth investigating.

The second consideration is that Gandhi is famous for his stance on non-violence. His tolerance and kindness for others marked him out as an especially gentle and kind person. If God is love, then indeed Gandhi proved with his actions his love of God.

Years after the bathrobe episode, I had another experience; it was Good Friday and I was in church. The crucifix was laid in front of the altar and there was a group of women around it crying and kissing the feet of Jesus. "How they love him I thought to myself enviously, they love him much more than I do." I heard the voice of Jesus in my head saying, *yes they love me, but they do not obey me.*

That experience convinced me that it is so much more important to practise the love that Jesus taught, rather than just attend church and worship Him.

What was it that procured the robber who was crucified with Jesus a place in heaven? Was it the fact that he believed Jesus to be the Son of God, was it the admission of his guilt and presumed repentance, or was it the kindness professed to Jesus after the harsh words of his companion? (Luke 23v39-43) I believe that it was the latter.

12

One day, whilst driving my sons to their swimming lesson I said to Saint Michael, "Don't ever ask me to sacrifice any of my children because I'll tell you right now the answer's no." I was thinking of the story of Isaac being offered in sacrifice by his father Abram (Genesis 22: 1-*13 Some time later God tested Abraham. he said to him, 'Abraham!'*

'Here I am,' he replied. Then God said, 'Take your son, your only son, Isaac, whom you love, and go to the region of Moriah. Sacrifice him there as a burnt offering on one of the mountains I will tell you about.'

Early the next morning Abraham got up and saddled his donkey. He took with him two of his servants and his son Isaac. When he had cut enough wood for the burnt offering, he set out for the place God had told him about. On the third day Abraham looked up and saw the place in the distance. He said to his servants, 'Stay here with the donkey, while I and the boy go over there. We will worship and then we will come back to you.'

Abraham took the wood for the burnt offering and placed it on his son Isaac and he himself carried the fire and the knife. As the two of them went on together, Isaac spoke up and said to his father Abraham, 'Father?'

'Yes my son?' Abraham replied.

'The fire and wood are here,' Isaac said, 'but where is the lamb for the burnt offering?'

Abraham answered, 'God himself will provide the lamb for the burnt offering, my son.' And the two of them went on together.

When they reached the place God had told him about. Abraham built an altar there and arranged the wood on it. He bound his son Isaac and laid him on the altar, on top of the wood. Then he reached out his hand and took the knife to slay his son.

But the angel of the Lord called out to him from heaven, 'Abraham! Abraham!'

'Here I am,' he replied.

'Do not lay a hand on the boy,' he said, ' do not do anything to him. Now I know that you fear God, because you have not withheld from me your son, your only son.'

Abraham looked up and there in a thicket he saw a ram caught by its horns. He went over and took the ram and sacrificed it as a burnt offering instead of his son.

Saint Michael smiled and said, *in reality, Isaac was never in any danger; it was all a question of priorities.* Abram was 100 years old when Isaac was born. He had given up all hope of ever having an heir from Sara, when his wildest dreams finally came true. Before the birth of Isaac, Abram had been in constant fellowship with God. His first act on awakening every morning was praying to God. During the day he was in constant conversation with God. His last thoughts at night were directed towards God. Then Isaac was born and everything changed. He was infatuated with his new son. As soon as he woke his thoughts were now directed towards Isaac. During the day he was obsessed with thoughts about Isaac, Isaac, Isaac, planning his future, worrying about his health, teaching him and fantasising about his future greatness. God needed clarification; was *He* still the focal point in Abram's life, or had Isaac usurped him? If the first hypothesis were true, then Abram would obey God and offer his son in sacrifice. God had no intention of allowing any harm to come to Isaac; He intervened at the last minute as is written in the Bible. If the second hypothesis were true however, Abram would never have agreed to sacrifice him. He would have swept him up in his arms and ran to the far corners of the earth in order to save him.

Every person has a focal point or if you prefer it a first priority, said Saint Michael. *The first priority of an alcoholic is a bottle of whiskey, the first priority of a drug addict is a syringe, and a newborn baby's focus is his mother's breast, the moon orbits around the earth, what is your first priority Norma?*

That question flipped me out. I didn't know. What was my first priority? It took me months of heart-searching, self-analysis, probing self-questioning before I came up with my answer. I would have liked to have been able to say, "Lord, you are my first priority," but I eventually realised that the sordid truth was much more basic. I discovered that my own economical security was what was really paramount in my life. What a hypocrite I was, and still am.

What a difference between Isaac and my sons. Isaac just passively allowed his father to sacrifice him. He probably jumped up on the wood all by himself to facilitate things for his father. His father, being at least 107 years old would have been too weak to have done it himself. Why didn't Isaac just run away? That episode in the Bible tells a lot about the mentality at that time. Children just believed emphatically in everything their parents said or did. They didn't question anything. It must have been very easy being a parent in those days, with no cinema, TV or spouse to undermine your authority.

At one time, I was disciplining my son Bengy and ordered him to go to his room; he was grounded. His parting shot over his shoulder before leaving the room was pissy pants. After we had become friends again I asked him about the remark and to my horror learned that because he had seen adverts on TV about sanitary towels, he had deducted that women were incontinent. At that point, I was forced to make a decision, either to allow him to continue his erroneous assumption, or give him the facts of life. He was seven at the time; he still believed in Santa Claus; he was far too young for a biology lesson.

Parents might underestimate the impact that TV has on their children in our western societies. A sit-com like Will and Grace makes an adult audience laugh, but just imagine what influence it could have on a crazy-mixed-up teenage boy. The homosexual young men in the series are portrayed as cool, exciting roll models; it might even give the impression that people can choose whatever sexual orientation they want to, which is ludicrous to my mind (or is it so ludicrous, what about bi-sexual people, where do they fit in?) but not to that of an adolescent who wants desperately to be admired.

When I was young, homosexual men and women were stigmatised, a shameful attitude, which was held by the majority of the population. Fortunately, down the years, people became more tolerant but now I have the impression that the mood is exaggerated in the other direction and that homosexuality is considered as an alternative option.

I know that there are some instances where homosexuality is caused by a physical dysfunction, but in the overwhelming majority of cases, it is psychological. Just as in anorexia the brain convinces itself that it is wrong to eat, sometime in childhood the brain of a homosexual convinces itself that its body is of the wrong gender.

I asked Saint Michael whether he was masculine or feminine. I was puzzled; he was portrayed as masculine by the church, yet when he spoke to me his voice was feminine. *Neither,* was the reply, *I am neither masculine nor feminine because I have no desire to possess or be possessed.*

****

I was late for church; I stepped into some dog's dirt but didn't realise it until I had already entered the church and was kneeling in the pew. I was dismayed; everything that happened to me in the physical was a projection of what was happening to me in the spiritual. I cried out to Saint Michael, "What have I done wrong? In what way have I defiled God's house?" I felt real anguish.

Weeks later I was asked to accompany a visiting priest to that church; I happily complied. I discovered months later, quite by chance that he was a homosexual.

In the beginning, the sexual act between Adam and Eve was considered a sacred ceremony. Today, casual sex has trivialised that concept beyond all recognition. There is hardly any similarity between the flippant attitude of today towards love making and the profound religious significance it once had. Our physical bodies are temples for the Holy Spirit and as such should be treated with reverence.

13

Jesus' ministry began at a wedding in Cana where he turned the water into wine. (John 2v1-11) The idea of writing this book was planted in my mind by Saint Michael at a wedding ceremony in Milan.

I'd made an appointment with a group of friends to meet at a church at 10 o'clock Saturday morning. There was to be a special mass; nobody turned up except me. I was at the wrong church. While I was waiting, preparations for a wedding were taking place. I decided to stay for the service; there was not enough time for me to go to the other church for Holy Mass. I wasn't exactly in my best outfit; I'd come straight from work. I decided to sit at the very back of the church by myself, far away from the invited guests.

Days before, I'd received a letter from my mother telling me that she was writing a book. That same day, a client had given me a gift of a book that she had written. "It must be an epidemic," I thought, "I hope it's not infectious."

I was puzzled; it was strange that I had mistaken the church. I bent down to rummage in my bag for my bible. It was dark in the back of the church and by mistake I extracted a book of the prophet Isaiah that I had bought the previous day. I opened it up at random; chapter 39 revealed itself. It spoke of showing everything to representatives of the king of Babylon. I didn't know what that meant so I made another attempt to pull out my bible from my very capacious bag. This time I succeeded and when I opened it at random, Isaiah chapter 39 appeared again. That could not have been a coincidence. The possibility of the same verses revealing themselves from two different books in two successive random attempts is virtually non-existent.

At that time Merodach-Baladan son of Baladan king of Babylon sent Hezekiah letters and a gift, because he had heard of his illness and recovery.

Hezekiah received the envoys gladly and showed them what was in his store houses- the silver, the gold, the spices, the fine oils, his entire armoury and everything found among his treasures. There was nothing in his palace or in all his kingdom that Hezekiah did not show them.

Then Isaiah the prophet went to King Hezekiah and asked, 'What did those men say, and where did they come from?'

'From a distant land,' Hezekiah replied. 'They came to me from Babylon.'

The prophet asked, 'What did they see in your palace?'

'They saw everything in my palace,' Hezekiah said. 'There is nothing among my treasures that I did not show them.'

Then Isaiah said to Hezekiah, 'Hear the word of the Lord Almighty: The time will surely come when everything in your palace, and all that your fathers have stored up until this day, will be carried off to Babylon. Nothing will be left, says the Lord. And some of your descendants, your own flesh and blood who will be born to you, will be taken away, and they will become eunuchs in the palace of the king of Babylon.'

'The word of the Lord you have spoken is good', Hezekiah replied. For he thought, 'There will be peace and security in my lifetime.'

I closely studied the text and it suddenly dawned on me, I was being asked to reveal all of my experiences in a book. I was dismayed; I'm not the literary type. Then Saint Michael explained that just as the bride was pledging to love honour and obey her new husband in the wedding ceremony, God was asking me to love honour and obey him. Writing this book is part of that pledge. Years later, in a different country, in a different language, I am honouring that pledge.

Nobody likes to reveal their innermost emotions to complete strangers; I know I don't, especially the murky regions of my heart. I decided therefore that if ever I did write the book, I would leave out the more compromising details.

That night I dreamt that I was outside Dino's house. Dino was a bricklayer that my husband had given some work to not long ago. He was the type of person that always looked for the double meaning in words, told dirty jokes and had an unhealthy interest in anything sexual. In the dream I was planting geraniums in his basement window box. He came over to me and reaching out pulled up all of the geraniums and threw them away. He then turned to me and said, "I haven't much light to start with and you'll block out even more with those fancy flowers."

I awoke and Saint Michael explained the meaning of the dream. The book that I was to write was to be aimed at people who had never opened a bible, had never frequented church services and had no notion of anything spiritual. I was to reveal all of my experiences, all that lay in my heart especially the murky corners of it. I was not to dress it up with "fancy flowers" because the spiritual truths in this book would, for some people, be their only means of spiritual enlightenment.

14

I was reluctant to have sex with my husband, knowing that there were other beings around watching. One night Saint Michael was in the middle of explaining something to me when suddenly he stopped and I saw him leaving the house through the front door. I was perplexed until my husband came into the room a few minutes later, then I realised that that was Saint Michael's way of letting me know that we were alone in the moments of intimacy.

You can imagine the horror I felt years later, one night while my husband was making love to me, to hear the voice of the Holy Spirit telling me to stop moving, to be still. It certainly froze me in my tracks. Even now, I still can't see what is sinful about participating with enthusiasm in love making with your legitimate husband in the classical position. If that is considered offensive, goodness knows what is thought about more hard-core sex.

****

The devil definitely exists. I've seen him on three occasions. The first time was in my bedroom. I was just dropping off to sleep and there he was, just his face. It was green and held a bored expression of supercilious contempt. At the same time a cat meowed and a serpent contorted under the blankets. Even my husband heard the meowing and asked me if we had acquired a cat. I was terrified and the next morning ran to my parish for holy water. I put it into a vaporiser and went all around the house squirting it in every nook and cranny.

The next time, he visited me in my kiosk at work. I'd had no clients all day and was depressed. I needed to talk to a friend and as this was in the days before I had a mobile phone, I crossed the road to the phone booth. I was making the call when I saw a big swanky car pull up in front of my kiosk. The chauffeur got out and walked all around the kiosk looking for someone to serve him. I quickly put down the phone and raced back across the road. Too late, he was back in the car and pulling away before I could attract his attention. I was so disappointed. Money was scarce that year and I couldn't afford to lose clients like that. I started to cry with disappointment as I saw the car pull up in front of my colleague's kiosk and watched as she compiled a huge bouquet of long stemmed roses. I complained to Saint Michael in no uncertain terms that I thought it unfair to be taunted in this way. *It isn't us*, he replied, *it is Satan.* Just then a woman appeared and asked me to look after her mother's grave every week. I happily signed her up as a new client.

The third time Satan paid me a visit was some years later. I had just got into bed; I wasn't even sleepy; in fact I was wide-awake. On closing my eyes, I saw an animated drawing of a woman masturbating. I was flabbergasted; I didn't think it possible for the devil to be so explicit in inviting me to sin. I silently shouted for Saint Michael and the drawing disappeared.

15

When the boys grew a little, we moved to the countryside just outside of Milan and both my husband and I started doing voluntary work with a community of drug-addicted youths. It was actually a pre-community; it took young men straight from the streets and gently gave them a routine before sending them onto stricter organisations best suitable for their needs. Mothers whose sons were addicted had set up the project. At that time my sons were too small to have problems with drugs, but little did I know what the future held in store for us.

That is how we met Mario. Mario had run away from the community he had been sent to and had asked my husband for help. The agreement reached between them was that he worked and lived with us and he kept off drugs. He didn't keep his part of the bargain and he eventually ended up in prison; I used to visit him every week. On one of the visits (his birthday) he was quite tipsy. He told me an episode that had happened to him in the prison that he would never have revealed to me if he had been sober. For the first time I empathised with priests listening to confessions; how do you express disapproval of the act without rejecting the perpetrator? I think he was trying to shock me (he succeeded); he watched my reaction; I was very embarrassed. I didn't know how to respond and to my relief the bell sounded; the visit was over before I could reply.

All the way home after the visit I churned over in my mind what he had told me but I was still at a loss for words. I arrived home and turned on the television; to my surprise I heard an evangelical preacher telling a story, which was relevant to my dilemma.

A chicken farmer went on a mountaineering holiday and one day out climbing, he saw an eagle's nest with an egg in it. He stole it and when he returned to his farm put it under a brooding hen. It eventually hatched out like all of the other chicks but that is where the similarity ended. The others were cute fluffy yellow balls, capable of feeding themselves as soon as they hatched; he was blind, naked and utterly dependent on others for all of his needs. He survived however and eventually joined his "siblings" in the farmyard, aping them, eyes down, in their continuous search for food. One-day mother eagle flew over the farmyard and her beady eyes spotted her stolen chick. She emitted a heart-rending cry of recognition; her chick heard it and looking up to the sky for the first time instinctively knew that he was meant to be up there, soaring freely, high in the blue sky, not down there enclosed behind a wire fence. At first it was difficult; he had never exercised his wings, but with daily practice and after many aborted attempts; he finally managed to escape from his earthbound prison and allow himself to become that which he was meant to be all along, a proud magnificent, awe-inspiring bird, free to roam wherever he chose and do whatever he wanted to do.

I immediately sat down and wrote a letter to Mario. I narrated the story and then said that he was that chick. He had a choice; he could consider himself either an eagle or a chicken. If he considered himself a chicken, then he had done right in doing what he had done in the prison, because chickens did that sort of thing, but if he considered himself an eagle, then he had done wrong because the eagle is too noble a bird to behave like that.

I would like to be able to say that from that day forth he was a changed person, but in real life things don't happen as they do in fairy tales.

In my life as Jacob, Mario was Issachar, my sixth son. He reincarnated as Jonathan, my favourite son when I was Saul, the first king of Israel. We were together with Jesus when he was John, the favourite apostle and I was Mary Magdalene.

****

A young man of about 27 came to my kiosk one day to buy flowers. He was homeless and used to go round houses knocking on doors begging for money and he used to give, whoever gave him anything, a flower in exchange. I thought that was a sweet gesture and before long we became friends.

One day, just as I was closing, he appeared looking grey; he had a high temperature and was obviously ill. It was winter and bitterly cold. I told him to go over the road to the church (Saint Anthony's church in Milan functions like Saint Martin in the field, in London, giving homeless people clothing, food and access to medical facilities). He replied that he had already been there but had found it closed. I eventually took him home with me but before leaving I told him the rules, just one glass of wine each night with the evening meal, nothing else alcoholic allowed on the premises.

He never gave me any trouble until one night, about six months later he drank his glass of wine, while still eating the first course of the evening meal. I reminded him of the rules and said that he could only drink water with the rest of the meal. My husband interrupted me, scolding me for my lack of empathy and immediately poured out another glass of wine for Tino. That was it; his attitude changed immediately. He challenged me continuously after that and about a week later he left. He didn't recognise my authority any more. I was fuming with my husband until I realised that Saint Michael was using this episode to explain to me that, that was what was wrong with my family; my sons did not recognise my authority. Saint Michael said, *In the beginning, it's as if the pointer in Tino's brain was pointing to; 'what fantastic luck, warm house, clean sheets, all the food I can eat and the cherry on the cake is a glass of wine every evening as well.' After my husband's intervention, the pointer switched and pointed to, 'what rotten luck, just one miserly glass of wine per meal, I'm not standing for this.'*

It was at this point that I realised that I could never rectify the situation with my sons, with my husband continuously undermined my authority and that I would eventually be forced to leave.

Years later, in March 2000 about three months after my return to England, I suffered two heart attacks within fifteen days of one another and was in hospital for quite a while. None of my sons came over to visit me; that hurt.

16

When Bengy was 5 years old he caught meningitis and was very ill. "Why has this happened to me?" I ranted and raved at Saint Michael. *Thou shalt not kill* was the reply. A few days earlier the dog had given birth to two dead puppies and a third agonised for a few hours before dying. She had chosen my son's bed as her maternity ward. The reason why the puppies had been stillborn was because months earlier, when I realised that she had been covered, I immediately went to the vet and asked him to give her an injection to terminate her pregnancy. Obviously it hadn't been effective. That was when I realised that I was on instant karma.

****

God gives His children gifts. Once on the metro in Milan I got off at the wrong stop. As I walked up the steps to go out into the street, something lying on the steps twinkled in the lamplight and caught my eye. I didn't stop to pick it up because I was in a hurry; with getting off at the wrong stop I had further to go. I was halfway down the street when I remembered that in my dream of the night before I had picked something up from the ground. I retraced my steps and sure enough it winked at me again; it was still there. It was a beautiful pearl earring with a small diamond underneath the pearl. I knew it was a gift from God and asked Saint Michael what it meant. He told me that I had "found" a profound equilibrium. The pearl represented the sun, the diamond represented the stars and the moon was represented by the clasp that kept the earring in place.

Many years later a friend gave me a tiny phial containing a tear from a stone statue of the Blessed Virgin in Milan. I valued it immensely and was wondering how I could wear it on my person, just then I looked down and there at my feet was a hollow cone- shaped pendulum. I inserted the phial into it and it was exactly the right size; it just clicked into place.

17

It was 6 a.m. I received a telephone call from my brother-in-law; my sister had undergone an emergency caesarean operation the night before and one of the twins was stillborn. I rushed to the hospital and stayed with her until one of her friends came to visit. I left her to be comforted by her friend and went to find her two daughters. The nun on the ward advised me to start my search on the maternity ward where my sister had given birth the previous night.

The receptionist was very polite but coldly refused to allow me to see my dead niece. Whilst I was arguing with her, out of the corner of my eye I saw a male nurse carrying what was obviously a dead child. The receptionist had seen him as well and her tone changed as she tried to detain me by asking me to fill in a form. I started to back away slowly from the desk and then turned around and ran towards the door that the nurse had disappeared behind. The receptionist shouted at me to stop and ran from behind her desk to prevent me from following him but it was too late. By that time I was through the door, down the stairs and taking my darling niece from the arms of a bewildered nurse. "This is my niece," I informed him, "I'll carry her to wherever you are taking her." Then the door above opened and the receptionist started to shout and scream at me rules and regulations. I ignored her completely and staring the nurse straight in the eyes said, "Lead the way and I will follow." He hesitated for a moment then obviously seeing the determination written on my face led the way down the remainder of the stairs and into an underground corridor, which led to the morgue.

I hugged the baby to me and silently told her how much I loved her and how distressed I was at her death. She was cold, so very cold; it felt as if I were holding a block of ice to my bosom. We passed the underground bar where a crowd of hospital staff were on their break, so many of them that they spilled out into the corridor. They fell silent at the sight of our small procession and waited for us to pass by before continuing their morning chatter. Further on I caught sight of a sign pointing left for the hospital chapel. I deviated and heard the nurse running after me and shouting that I was going the wrong way. I opened the door to the chapel and the priest (I presumed it was the priest) came out of an adjoining door that led to his living quarters. He was still in his pyjamas and his face was covered in shaving cream. He hastily tried to wipe it clean with a towel he was carrying but didn't quite succeed. "Father," I said tearfully, "This is my niece; I would like you to bless her." He was wonderful. He prayed over her and blessed her and anointed her with holy water nearly drowning us all in the process. After the improvised ceremony had ended, I thanked him and obediently followed the nurse to the morgue where he allowed me to stay with her to recite my rosary.

The next few days I could feel her around me as I organised her funeral. Then one night I heard her call me mamma. Every night for the next three months her "foster mother" used to bring her to me and I could see myself pushing her in a pram to the local shops. I used to enjoy her visits and as soon as I felt her around me welcomed her by calling her my love or my darling. Then one night, inexplicably she replied, "I'm not your love, I'm my mamma's love." I replied, "Yes, but I'm still your favourite auntie aren't I?" She nodded coyly then she disappeared and I've not heard nor seen her since.

First consideration is that "someone" had revealed to her that I wasn't her mother and probably took her to bond with her parents and siblings after that.

Second consideration is that she grew much more quickly and was more advanced than her live twin. At the end of the three months, she looked and acted as a two or three year old child.

My mother was very puzzled when I told her this. Her argument was that as the autopsy had revealed that the organs of the baby were two thirds of the normal size, then it was probable that she had died in the womb when my sister was six months pregnant; and she should have been in heaven for the last three months not hanging around waiting to be born. My viewpoint was different. I have been taught that mothers provide the vehicle, God provides the engines; they are united at birth. The soul of the child, containing it's spiritual, emotional and mental bodies, hovers around it's pregnant mother until it is time for the birth when it enters it's new body with it's first breath. I sincerely believe that the soul of my niece was still trying to enter her assigned body when I came on the scene. Being unsuccessful, she then followed me. I was probably the launching pad from which she was projected into heaven (heaven being the sixth astral plane.) I don't know why or how; she might have felt the love emitting from me while I was carrying her body; it might have been the improvised ceremony in the chapel, I don't know. What has been confirmed for me in this experience is that the soul is definitely not in the body whilst it is still in the womb.

It was Saint Michael who pointed out to me the ethics of "Eating." I was watching a documentary on factory farming. At one end of the factory piglets were born; at the other they came out as packaged bacon. In between times, they had not felt the warmth of the sun on their skins, tasted natural food nor walked on green grass.

In another factory, eggs were hatched artificially by light bulbs; they ended up as dead chickens ready for the supermarkets. "Surely the owners of these factories are guilty of exploiting those animals," I thought. Saint Michael came through; *no they are only exploiting your demands for bacon and eggs.* "So it's wrong to eat meat?" I asked. Before the fall, not only Adam and Eve were vegetarians, but all of the animals were as well.

(Genesis 1:29...*Then God said, 'I give you every seed-bearing plant on the face of the whole earth and every tree that has fruit with seed in it. They will be yours for food. And to all the beasts of the earth and all the birds of the air and all the creatures that move on the ground-everything that has the breath of life in it –I give every green plant for food.' And it was so.)*

That was the beginning of a long journey for me. Every lent I was asked to relinquish a particular type of food. The first year it was meat; the second year it was fish, subsequently it was eggs, then dairy products and finally cooked vegetables.

At the same time Saint Michael introduced me to fasting. The first year I fasted on Fridays; the second year Fridays and Wednesdays the next year I added Mondays; subsequently I was fasting Mondays and Tuesdays, Thursdays and Fridays. In the end I was eating as much mixed salad as my body permitted at weekends. On fasting days I was allowed to eat as many oranges as I wanted to but drank only water.

During those years, I questioned the wisdom of such an extreme diet, but every time I "cheated" and ate anything other than an orange at the time I was supposed to be fasting, I was punished. My punishment was watching my son suffer. Since his meningitis Bengy had suffered from excruciating headaches accompanied by vomit. I noticed that these attacks occurred every time I disobeyed. Both Bengy and I had obviously conceded before our births to this arrangement but it was hard on both of us; on the other hand I knew we were both being cared for.

One day, in the cemetery, as I was tending a grave, a sparrow landed beside me and dropped a piece of brown bread on the tomb I was working on before flying off. I took that to mean that my body needed some brown bread; I dropped everything and rushed to the nearest bakery and was just in time to buy the last loaf of brown bread before it closed. Near the end I was very weak. "This is madness," I thought so I went to a coffee bar and ordered a fresh fruit salad. I was just about to put the first spoonful in my mouth when it was conveyed to me, *if you eat that; you will lock yourself out of paradise.* I put the spoon down and walked out. This happened on Thursday; on the following Saturday, I was so weak my legs buckled up under me so I crawled back to bed. "This is it," I thought, "I'm going to die." I had mixed feelings; I was sad about leaving my boys, but on the other hand I completely trusted Saint Michael. If he had guided me to this point, then even if I couldn't see the logic of it, he knew what he was doing as far as I was concerned.

While I was lying there I had a vision of two angels supporting a woman obviously dead as her head was lolling onto her left shoulder; was that me? All three were ascending (into heaven?) Then I saw the Holy Spirit in the form of a dove descending. Up until that time, on hearing of the descent of the Holy Spirit, I had imagined it to be like an ordinary dove, but it wasn't like that at all. It descended very slowly, tail first in a helical spiral resting every half circle, flapping its wings once each time. Silver sparks escaped from its body every time it flapped its wings. I can only describe its colour as snow sparkling in the moonlight. I eventually dropped off to sleep and when I awoke, two hours later, I was told that I could eat anything I wanted to, except meat and potatoes; I made a dash for the fridge. I can still remember the relish with which I ate my first yoghurt in years.

To this day I still can't figure out why it was necessary for me to suffer so much torment.

One day I was watching an old movie, Samson and Delilah. I was deliberating over the relevance of Samson's hair with his strength. "Samson's strength is in his hair," I mused, "and Jesus' power is in his blood. I wonder what my strength is related to." *Your saliva* was the reply.

19

It was the middle of the night and I was fast asleep. *Get up*, commanded Saint Michael. I dragged myself out of bed and knelt to pray. I was taken in spirit to a church; we stood standing in an aisle to the left of a row of pews. There were about ten to fifteen people kneeling in the pews and looking up, I saw the powerful arms of God with a well used coal bucket about to anoint them with what I can only describe as "dry water." "Oh boy, I want to get in on this," I exclaimed and jumped into the nearest pew. Saint Michael threw my cardigan in after me. Up until that experience, I had always imagined God doing His anointing with dainty gold and silver vessels.

****

Every day, even now, I consult the bible to see what God has to say to me. I pick it up then with eyes closed; I open it at random and read whatever meets my eye. On this particular occasion, I had opened it more or less in the middle; obviously God wanted to tell me something at the beginning of the bible because the pages just turned over and over by themselves until they stopped at Genesis 28: 10-22, Jacob's dream about the ladder and God's angels ascending and descending.

Jacob left Beersheba and set out for Haran. When he reached a certain place, he stopped for the night because the sun had set. Taking one of the stones there, he put it under his head and lay down to sleep. He had a dream in which he saw a stairway resting on the earth, with its top reaching to heaven, and the angels of God were ascending and descending on it. There above it stood the Lord and he said, 'I am the Lord, the God of your father Abraham and the God of Isaac. I will give you and your descendants the land on which you are lying. Your descendants will be like the dust of the earth, and you will spread out to the west and to the east, to the north and to the south. All peoples on earth will be blessed through you and your offspring. I am with you and will watch over you wherever you go, and I will bring you back to this land. I will not leave you until I have done what I have promised you.

When Jacob awoke from his sleep, he thought, 'Surely the Lord is in this place, and I was not aware of it.' He was afraid and said, 'How awesome is this place! This is none other than the house of God; this is the gate of heaven.'

Early the next morning Jacob took the stone that he had placed under his head and set it up as a pillar and poured oil on top of it. He called that place Bethel, though the city used to be called Luz.

Then Jacob made a vow, saying, 'If God will be with me and will watch over me on this journey I am taking and will give me food to eat and clothes to wear so that I return safely to my father's house, then the Lord will be my God and this stone that I have set up as a pillar will be God's house, and of all that you give me I will give you a tenth.'

****

Angels have a wonderful sense of humour. I had been told that stones behave more or less like plants (photosynthesis) absorbing energy from the planets during the day and emitting it at night. I decided to sleep with a flat rock under my pillow like Jacob at Bethel (Genesis 28:10-22). After a week of dreamless nights I complained to Saint Michael. That night I had a dream. I saw elegant courtiers of Luis 14th King of France, complete with powdered wigs and elegant tights ascending and descending a wide ornate staircase. (In Italian, the word for staircase and ladder is the same.)

I was sitting in a room on a potty; a friend from my adolescence was present; I evacuated two stools; I walked across the room and emptied the potty out of the window. A pack of howling dogs fought over them. I awoke and immediately started to ponder about what the dream might mean. I knew it was set in my teens because of the presence of my friend, but what did the two stools represent? One probably represented an illness that I had at that time; I used to have frequent blackouts. The doctor diagnosed epilepsy but I have my doubts. It still happens occasionally but much less frequently.

What the other stool represented was beyond my comprehension until I heard Saint Michael whisper, *masturbation*. I realised that the dream was an invitation to acknowledge past sins and then wave goodbye to them forever.

I had always masturbated from being a very young child; it was probably the only means by which I received love as a child, I certainly received very little from my parents; I can't recall a single instance of being kissed or cuddled by either one of them. I hadn't associated masturbation with sin; it gave me the comfort, the solace that somehow compensated for the lack of love from my parents. I continued to practice it right up to my marriage; I never considered it as sin until I was told it was by means of this dream.

20

I very rarely saw any of my defunct family. On one occasion I saw an old woman carrying a basket of eggs; I didn't recognise her as my grandmother until I received a telephone call from my mother in England, scolding me for having disturbed her. "If you're worried about the kids 'phone me," she said, "It's easier, anyway she recommends that you feed him with fresh eggs, that should do the trick." I had been worried about David not eating enough; my grandmother must have picked up my worried vibes.

The fact that I felt resentment towards my mother because she didn't love me as much as she did my siblings worried me; by this time I had learned enough to know that it hurt me more than it did her. I decided to do something about it; I planned to ask her to come with me on a holiday so that we could thrash it out.

One day I heard John Lennon singing his song "mother" on the radio, I couldn't help it, emotion swelled up inside of me and I started to sob uncontrollably. That night he visited me. His song had set off a sadness that probably reverberated with the sadness that he felt for his situation with his mother. The next night he returned again, this time with his mother. I think he wanted to comfort me by letting me know that it's never too late to patch up relationships. If we can't do it in this dimension, then we are obliged to do it in the next.

My mother was convinced that her twin soul was my son David, her grandson. I tend to agree with her because there were too many coincidences to account for otherwise. She came over to Italy to be present at his birth, (she had five Italian grandchildren but was present only for his birth.) She wanted to take him back with her to England and raise him as her own but I would not agree to it. She stayed five months and after she departed, David really showed signs of distress. I only realised later, that he was mourning my mother's absence. In a past life he had been King David and she Bethsheba (2 Samuel chapters 11.) Towards the end of her life she was convinced that she was working off David's karma for him; she felt that she had come to the end of her cycle of incarnations and was helping David with his. I disagreed.

My mother had a karmic relationship with practically all of her close relations. She was married to my father, who was the reincarnation of Uriah the Hittite, whom she as Bethsheba with king David had murdered, sending him to certain death (2 Samuel 11:2-17.) *One evening David got up from his bed and walked around on the roof of the palace. From the roof he saw a woman bathing. The woman was very beautiful and David sent someone to find out about her. The man said, 'Isn't this Bathsheba, the daughter of Eliam and the wife of Uriah the Hittite?' Then David sent messengers to get her. She came to him and he slept with her. (She had purified herself from her uncleanness.) Then she went back home. The woman conceived and sent word back to David, saying, 'I am pregnant.'*

So David sent this word to Joab: 'Send me Uriah the Hittite.' And Joab sent him to David. When Uriah came to him, David asked him how Joab was, how the soldiers were and how the war was going. Then David said to Uriah, 'Go down to your house and wash your feet.' So Uriah left the palace and a gift from the king was sent after him. But Uriah slept at the entrance to the palace with all his master's servants and did not go down to his house.

When David was told, 'Uriah did not go home,' he asked him, 'Haven't you just come from a distance? Why didn't you go home?'

Uriah said to David, 'The ark and Israel and Judah are staying in tents, and my master Joab and my lord's men are camping in the open fields. How could I go to my house and eat and drink and lie with my wife? As surely as you live, I will not do such a thing!'

Then David said to him, 'Stay here one more day, and tomorrow I will send you back.' So Uriah remained in Jerusalem that day and the next. At David's invitation, he ate and drank with him, and David made him drunk. But in the evening, Uriah went out to sleep on his mat among his master's servants; he did not go home.

In the morning David wrote a letter to Joab and sent it with Uriah. In it he wrote, 'Put Uriah in the front line where the fighting is fiercest. Then withdraw from him so that he will be struck down and die.'

So while Joab had the city under siege, he put Uriah at a place where he knew the strongest defenders were. When the men of the city came out and fought against Joab, some of the men in David's army fell; moreover, Uriah the Hittite was dead.)

My mother suffered terribly at the hands of my father; he was a very violent man; she paid that karmic debt back right up to the last penny.

She also had a karmic relationship with me. Five thousand years ago she had been my father Isaac. At that time I was Jacob and tricked him into giving me my brother's inheritance. *(Genesis chapter 27) When Isaac was old and his eyes were so weak that he could no longer see, he called for Esau his older son and said to him, 'My son.'*

'Here I am' he answered.

Isaac said, 'I am now an old man and don't know the day of my death. Now then, get your weapons-your quiver and bow-and go out to the open country to hunt some wild game for me. Prepare me the kind of tasty food I like and bring it to me to eat so that I may give you my blessing before I die'

Now Rebekah was listening as Isaac spoke to his son Esau. When Esau left for the open country to hunt game and bring it back, Rebekah said to her son Jacob, 'Look, I overheard your father say to your brother, Esau. Bring me some game and prepare me some tasty food to eat, so that I may give you my blessing in the presence of the Lord before I die. Now my son, listen carefully to what I tell you: Go out to the flock and bring me two choice young goats, so that I can prepare some tasty food for your father, just the way he likes it. Then take it to your father to eat, so that he may give you his blessing before he dies.'

Jacob said to Rebekah his mother, 'But my brother Esau is a hairy man and I'm a man with smooth skin. What if my father touches me? I would appear to be tricking him and would bring down a curse on myself rather than a blessing.'

His mother said to him, 'My son, let the curse fall on me. Just do what I say. Go and get them for me.'

So he went and got them and brought them to his mother and she prepared some tasty food, just the way his father liked it. Then Rebekah took the best clothes of Esau her older son which she had in the house, and put them on her younger son Jacob. She also covered his hands and the smooth part of his neck with the goatskins. Then she handed to her son Jacob the tasty food and the bread she had made.

He went to his father and said, 'My father!'

'Yes my son?' he answered. 'Who is it?'

Jacob said to his father, 'I am Esau, your firstborn. I have done as you told me. Please sit up and eat some of my game so that you may give me your blessing.'

Isaac asked his son, 'How did you find it so quickly, my son?'

'The Lord your God gave me success,' he replied

Then Isaac said to Jacob, 'Come near so I can touch you, my son, to know whether you really are my son Esau or not.'

Jacob went close to his father Isaac, who touched him and said, 'The voice is the voice of Jacob but the hands are the hands of Esau.' He didn't recognise him for his hands were hairy, like those of his brother Esau; so he blessed him.

'Are you really my son Esau?' he asked.

'I am.' He replied.

Then he said, 'My son, bring me some of your game to eat so that I may give you my blessing.'

Jacob brought it to him and he ate; and he brought some wine and he drank. Then his father Isaac said to him, 'Come here my son and kiss me.' So he went to him and kissed him. When Isaac caught the smell of his clothes, he blessed him and said, 'Ah. The smell of my son is like the smell of a field that the Lord has blessed. May God give you of heaven's dew and of earth's richness- an abundance of grain and new wine. May nations serve you and peoples bow down to you. Be lord over your brothers, and may the sons of your mother bow down to you. May those who curse you be cursed and those who bless you be blessed.'

In that life, my mother as Isaac preferred my brother Esau to me. In this life she reiterated that preference; Esau is reincarnated as one of my brothers. Incidentally, his wife in this life is the reincarnation of Rebekah, my mother of five thousand years ago. In this life, she and my mother didn't exactly hit it off, but she and I bond wonderfully.

Even though I had often accused her of not loving me as much as she did my siblings, my mother would never admit it. I am sure that while she was alive she convinced herself that that was the truth. After her death though, in the astral plane, she was forced to face the negative emotion that she felt towards me and deal with it.

It was a few months after her death, about 5.am; I suddenly heard her voice, "I've always preferred the boys to you." It didn't upset me, in fact it made me smile; at long last she was admitting the truth. Shortly after that episode, I was on my way to college to attend my massage class when I realised that my nails were too long. My tutor was very severe about nail lengths. I popped into Boots with the intention of buying a pair of nail scissors. I was busy selecting the type I wanted and thinking that it was a pity that I was obliged to buy another pair when I had numerous pairs at home. Her voice came through loud and clear, "I should think so too with all of the pairs of scissors that I left you." "You're right," I replied, "But it can't be helped."

I could feel her presence around me as I walked up to the college. "Are you following me?" I asked. "Yes," was the reply. "Why?" I continued. She hesitated a moment before replying, "Because I'm learning to love you." I'm ashamed to tell you my response but for the sake of accuracy I must. "If you didn't f…ing manage it in the fifty-seven years we were down here together, I can't see you f...ing succeeding now. F… off." A few days later I visited her grave and apologised. I've never seen or heard from her since.

21

I once saw two leopards walking up and down the long narrow corridor in my third floor flat in Milan. I only found out the meaning of that, after my experience at Findhorn.

Findhorn is a spiritual community on the northeast coast of Scotland. Eileen and Peter Caddy founded it originally, planting vegetables to feed their family. It evolved into a magical garden where giant cabbages and eight-foot delphiniums grew in abundance. More recently, it has transformed itself into a community catering for the spiritual needs of its visitors. I decided to go there to face the negative emotions I felt towards my mother (she was still alive at this time). At first I believed that it would be appropriate for my mother to be there with me but according to Saint Michael, it was I that should relinquish the resentment (how dare she not love me) not her; she was oblivious to the enormity of my problem.

Before leaving Milan, I had filled in the forms and enclosed the fee but on arrival there was no trace of my booking and there were no vacancies on the course that I had chosen, what now? A woman who was staying at the same hotel as I was, told me of another course, so I enrolled on it, my only other option was returning home with nothing achieved.

The woman holding the course was an American Shaman. She looked like any ordinary businesswoman, but when she opened her briefcase and extracted her rattle, drums and magical stones instead of typewritten A4 sheets of paper, there was no doubt of her identity. She started the session by sending us all out into the garden to find an object, which would introduce us to our inner personality. "It's not you that will find the object, it's the object which will find you," was her parting words to us as we all filed out into the chilly evening air. Twenty minutes later we were all sitting in a circle with our treasures in front of us. My object was a piece of bark that had fallen off the trunk of a tree; it personified perfectly the feeling of detachment from mainstream society that had engulfed me recently.

The first few days were spent in dealing with the negativity that the whole group needed to be released from; every person present had his or her own personal demons to confront, but the last few days made up for all of the pain and anguish we had endured up until then.

She explained to us that the totem poles found in the villages of the American Indian camps were not dedicated to pagan gods as originally assumed by the white man, but were a tribute to the inner animals of the person who had erected it. She said that we all have animals attached to the seven chakras along our spine. We were told to lie down on the floor and she drummed us into a state of relaxation. She started with the third eye chakra; I could see people around me writing down what animal had appeared to them, none came to me; I had already met my third eye animal, the leopard; chakra animals appear only once in a lifetime. She then systematically took us down all of the rest of the chakra points ending with the crown chakra, because this animal rules the other six. My animals are, leopard, water buffalo, white dove, monkey, cobra and mouse all ruled over by a white circus horse. It was very exciting being introduced to the animals that together make up your character. The leopard represented intuition, (leopards can see in the dark) the water buffalo patience, the white dove peace, the monkey my emotions, the cobra the ability to strike out unexpectedly when danger is perceived, the mouse the love of stability, all ruled over by a white circus horse that represented a sense of humour. Everybody in the room was introduced to all of their animals except a nineteen-year-old boy who had recently been in a psychiatric ward and was still on medication.

The next session was spent in healing any animal that was injured. This is what happened to me. I was walking in a wood with all of my animals when we came to a clearing. The monkey lay down listlessly and all of the other animals formed a circle around it. At once different coloured faces zoomed down towards the monkey missing him by inches before zooming off again into the distance. "What are those faces doing to him," I asked indignantly. *They are his negative emotions bidding him farewell before leaving him,* a voice said. *The red one is uncontrolled rage, the green one is envy, the yellow one is cowardice; he is being healed.* After the last face had departed the monkey jumped up onto the back of the circus horse and performed all sorts of acrobats and pirouettes while the horse paraded round and round just like in a circus; the other animals applauded.

I would just like to add that it has been revealed to me that Peter Caddy is the reincarnation of Abraham, my grandfather in my first life. Eileen is the reincarnation of Sarah, his wife. When Peter left and went to America to live with his son born to him by a young

American woman, Eileen was paying back the karma she created 5000 years ago when as Sarah, she deprived Abraham the joys of seeing his son grow up by insisting that Hagar and her child be driven out into the desert (Genesis 21:10.) *And she* (Sarah) *said to Abraham, 'Get rid of that slave woman and her son, for that slave woman's son will never share in the inheritance with my son Isaac.'*

****

I looked out of my third floor flat window one day and saw a woman running across the square, before my very eyes she turned into an ostrich.

****

Whilst talking to a client one day, she inadvertently spat all over me. She apologised profusely and admitted that it often happened to her. Then before my very eyes she turned into a camel.

****

I was once in a traffic jam in Milan. Everyone was tooting their horn and gesturing at each other, it was utter chaos. Suddenly as I watched, every driver turned into a different animal; the two main drivers, who had caused the problem, turned into wildebeests.

****

While I was visiting Findhorn, I was introduced to many different books on white witchcraft. I bought two or three to take back to Italy with me together with an elongated quartz crystal (my wand), which I used to wear around my neck, contained in a cloth pocket that I had made especially for it.

On the last day there, I slipped and fell down a flight of stairs; my bottom bounced off every stair and was sore for weeks after. I still didn't connect my physical fall to my spiritual fall into witchcraft until my mother pointed it out to me. I repented, got rid of the books but still kept the crystal round my neck until one day while having a pee in a Turkish loo, it slipped out of its pocket and I heard a large "Plop" as it fell into the water all by itself.

I took the hint and have steered clear of witchcraft, white or any other colour ever since.

****

I was abruptly awoken in the middle of the night by a witch trying to rip open my stomach with her nails; they were more like the talons of a bird of prey. I screamed silently to Saint Michael for help and she immediately disappeared.

****

22

It has always saddened me to read in the bible that two bears mauled 42 youths only because they dared to taunt a man of God. (2 kings 2:23-*24 from there Elisha went up to Bethel. As he was walking along the road, some youths came out of the town and jeered at him. 'Go on up, you baldhead!' they said. 'Go on up, you baldhead!' He turned round, looked at them and called down a curse on them in the name of the Lord. Then two bears came out of the woods and mauled forty-two of the youths.*) I would have thought that a man of God would have been evolved enough to take sneers and jeers in his stride; but God does avenge his chosen ones.

One Sunday, in 1994, I was told that my son David had been involved in an accident. He and his friend both aged 18, had been on a scooter and had been knocked down by a car. David broke his right tibia; his friend was unscathed. Eight years later, his leg was still broken; it has just recently healed.

Three days before the accident, David had been very disrespectful to me, hurting me to the core. I know these two incidents are related. I did not consciously curse him as Elisha did those youths, but I believe at a subconscious level I might have. I know I experienced anger and humiliation.

In my quest to find a surgeon capable of healing David's leg, I eventually found someone whom I thought was competent; the only trouble being that he was asking a prohibitive fee for his private clinic. He also worked in a state hospital but the waiting list was six months. Driving home after the visit I started to pray to Saint Metatron. Saint Metatron is the Archangel that reigns over all of the archangels. Tradition has it that he walked the earth as Enoch (Genesis 5:21-24.) and was so favoured by God that after his death he was promoted to that seat of excellence. I asked him to lead me to a winning scratch card, after all it was for a good cause, David's leg; the money wouldn't be spent on anything trivial. I went to a bar and bought my scratch card; I was convinced that I would win; I did not. I threw the card away in disgust and started to pray (complain) to Saint Metatron. His reply was, *take your gold necklace and give it to the surgeon.* "I can't do that," I said, "It's bribery." *You are looking at the problem from the wrong viewpoint*, he replied, *just imagine that David's leg is held to ransom. You would pay a ransom for the leg of your son would you not?*

A few days later I paid another visit to the surgeon and asked him to put David on the waiting list. He made a note in his diary and I slipped him the necklace before leaving. "A small gift for your wife," I said. He thanked me without unwrapping the gift. A week later I received a letter from his secretary informing me that David's name had been put on the waiting list and that I would be hearing from her at the appropriate time. I went ballistic with Saint Metatron; not only had I not gained any time; I had gambled away an expensive piece of jewellery as well. *Have faith* was the only reply I received. A week later, David had a very high temperature, 40 degrees centigrade. I was in a dilemma, I had already taken him away from his former surgeon, but he had not yet been accepted by his new one. I took the bull by the horns and drove him (three hours) to the state hospital where the new surgeon worked. He wasn't there; it was his day off. The doctor on the A&È who examined David's leg immediately accepted him as an emergency admission.

23

David's leg still wasn't healing. The new team, headed by a brilliant surgeon was doing its best but after more than a year of errors committed by the other hospital, the leg was not responding as it should have. I'd heard that Monsignor Melingo was holding a healing mass just outside of Milan on Saturday afternoon; I decided to ask permission to take David home for the weekend. The hospital gave their consent but David although eager to come home for the weekend, refused to accompany me to the healing mass. "No mass, no weekend at home," I threatened. He grudgingly accepted a compromise, he would attend the mass but from 6pm on Saturday, his time was his own. He immediately telephoned a girl he was keen on and made a date with her for 8pm. I was reasonably satisfied with the deal we had struck; the masses of Monsignor Melingo usually started at 3pm and lasted until about 5pm at the most 5.30pm which gave me ample time to complete my mission.

We arrived at the venue in plenty of time only to discover that Monsignor Melingo had been detained and the mass would probably be postponed. "Great," was David's response to the news, "It's no good hanging around here, let's go." "Hang on," I replied, "Give me time to think this through." I sat down on a bench to mull over my options trying to ignore the glee written all over David's face. He sat down beside me to rest his leg when a co-worker of Monsignor Melingo passed by and commented on the heavy iron case supporting David's broken leg. I explained that his leg had been broken for well over a year and was giving no signs of healing. I added that I was convinced that the source of the problem was not physical. He looked at us both intensely for a moment then told us to follow him. He took us to a small room to the right, just off the main hall where the mass was to be held and told us to wait there; it was full of troubled people. Everybody in that room was waiting for a private audience with Monsignor Melingo. I could feel David's nervousness and gave him my rosary to hold; for once in his life he didn't refuse it. I closed my eyes and started to pray, David started chatting to a very pretty teenage girl sitting next to him.

Monsignor Melingo arrived about an hour later, I knew of his arrival before seeing him because of the reaction of shouts and screams from people all around us. Fifteen minutes later we were all ushered into an even smaller room; Monsignor Melingo was sitting at the far end; we were near the end of the queue but could see and hear everything that was happening. One by one people filed past him and told him their troubles; he prayed over them or exorcised them whichever was appropriate. Then it was the turn of the pretty teenage girl who had been sitting beside David. Her mother explained to Monsignor Melingo that her mother-in-law had recently died and since then her daughter had twice tried to commit suicide. She added that her husband had been estranged from his mother while she had been alive but had still inherited all of her money at her death. She felt that this was the problem but her husband refused to relinquish his inheritance. Monsignor Melingo ordered the girl to kneel in front of him but she refused and it took two strong men to force her to her knees. He questioned her and abusive language poured out of her mouth; gone was the sweet voice of a normal teenager, replaced by the cackling of an old hag, deriding Jesus and praising satanic masses. I looked at David to see his reaction and saw that he was greatly affected by the whole scenario. He was sweating profusely and had an expression of horror and disbelief on his face. Eventually it was our turn and after hearing our story Monsignor Melingo blessed us and prayed over David's leg.

As soon as we had left the building, reaction set in. David started to heave with emotion; he was sobbing; no tears, just sobs; I was distressed to see him like that and apologised to him for having put him through that ordeal. I had taken him there for his leg, hoping that the healing mass would kick-start the healing process, but in retrospect, I'm sure that the real reason behind the scenes was to put him off dabbling in the occult.

24

After reading the book of Job in the Old Testament, I was struck with the similarities between his family and mine; both dysfunctional. *His sons used to take turns holding feasts (Job 1v 4)* my sons seem to be continuously at some rave or other.

Early in the morning he (Job) would sacrifice a burnt offering for each of them, thinking, "Perhaps my children have sinned and cursed God in their hearts."(Job1v5) It's impossible to count the numerous occasions that I have implored God to forgive my sons for their attitude towards Him.

(Job's)... sons and daughters were feasting and drinking wine when suddenly a mighty wind swept in from the desert and struck the four corners of the house. It collapsed on them and they are dead. (Job 1v19) In my opinion, David and Bengy are spiritually dead. They started off as altar boys and both of them were believers until they fell in with the group of friends that they still frequent 12 years later. They both have children to girls belonging to that group.

As if that wasn't enough, Job was then afflicted with painful sores all over his body. My health was affected with the worry and stress caused by the behaviour of my sons, two heart attacks and diabetes.

I only hope that the final outcome of my ordeal is as happy as the outcome of Job's story.

****

Mario used to steal from me to feed his habit, after it happened for the umpteenth time I was contemplating sending him back to jail. I didn't want to but I thought that he should have shown more gratitude, after all, house arrests was infinitely better than a crowded Italian prison. I was complaining to God about his conduct and enumerating all of the reasons why, in my opinion, it would be better if he went. "So, what do you want me to do?" I concluded. *Give him a kiss*, Saint Michael replied.

I obeyed; through clenched teeth but it was definitely a kiss.

25

I was at work, at the kiosk selling flowers when I saw the Holy Trinity. I didn't see their upper bodies; each was wearing a different pin striped suit; navy blue, brown and grey. They asked me to feed their children. I promised to look after anyone they sent to me, if they would look after my sons. The next day, and every weekday after that, up to the last day before I left for England, I used to go to the supermarket and buy bread, ham and cheese. Through the day I used to make up the sandwiches and then after work, I used to go to the central station of Milan and hand them out to the dropouts and drug addicts that frequented the place. My husband and I also gave hospitality over the years to various young men whom we thought had been sent by God for us to look after. Many years later when I realised that two of my three sons were addicted to heroin, I felt bitterness towards God. I felt that He had not kept His part of the bargain.

****

It was noon and I was lying on the bed trying to persuade my baby into taking his usual afternoon nap when I saw a huge pink eye hovering above me. I still can't figure out what that meant.

****

I once saw a Chinese gentleman, he wrote in the air, "Ask me a question." I had a migraine at the time so very abruptly told him to leave me alone. He immediately vanished and although I've apologised to him many times, He's never ever come back to see me. That was an opportunity that I regret wasting.

****

During the period that I was depressed, one of the things that used to frighten me was seeing a sea of hands helping me out of bed every morning. Now I know that it was to gently encourage me to get up and let me know that I had help when I needed it, but back then, it just used to freak me out.

****

At the beginning of my spiritual tuition from Saint Michael, I was overawed by the piety of others. I once attended a prayer meeting at the house of a very wealthy couple. It was the first time that I had heard prayers recited with such loquacity; I was very impressed. That night in a dream, I saw the grand piano that had been in one of the sitting rooms floating on a sea of sewage.

****

I went through a bout of depression some time ago. I'd seen so many fine young men die of overdoses, or aids or whatever, that even just seeing a discarded needle in the street used to set me off crying. I then had this vision. I saw an enormous fly's eye resting on a cart, which was moving extremely slowly through the streets of Milan. Then the voice, *God works slowly but is all seeing, all knowing.*

****

Saint Michael told me that we had been together since twelve years before my birth in 1944.

****

One ounce of conscious sin weighs more than one ton of sin committed unknowingly.

****

I was asked never to cut my hair, to stop wearing makeup and to keep my fingernails cut very short.

26

In the very beginning when I started to have these experiences I was convinced that I was insane. Nothing of that kind had ever happened to me before and having no one to confide in, I came to the logical conclusion that I was losing my mind. I became very depressed; joy was absent from my life. Saint Michael must have been worried about me because one evening awake in bed, I suddenly had the sensation that I was in the last seat of the last carriage of a train, which had just entered a tunnel at an enormous speed. As I watched out of the rear window, daylight, shining in from the opening of the tunnel receded until it was just a speck of light then there was complete darkness. I screamed silently, "Stop, I don't want to." The train slowed down before coming to a halt and then picked up speed again and was soon hurtling down the tracks at a fantastic speed in the opposite direction. The spot of light appeared and then grew bigger and bigger until the train finally emerged from the tunnel. I now know that I was a fainthearted fool not to continue; who knows what wonderful encounters were waiting for me on the other side of that tunnel. On the other hand, if I had allowed the train to continue, I might not have needed the intervention of Carl Jung, the famous psychoanalyst, to convince me that I was not insane and that would have deprived me of an extremely powerful experience.

A few nights later in a dream, I saw myself talking to a grey haired gentleman wearing a light blue jacket. The next day, I glanced in the window of a bookshop and saw a book with a light blue jacket; I knew that I was meant to read it. It was that book, "Memories Dreams and Reflections" that convinced me that I might not be insane after all. It was thanks to Carl Jung and his experiences written in the book, many similar to mine, and his gentle discrete interventions, that convinced me that there might be another explanation after all for everything that was happening to me. During the reading of the book I remember saying aloud to him, "Thank you for the help you are giving me, I'm sorry you're dead, I would have liked to have met you. Then again, even if you were still on this earth, we would never have met because we are socially and geographically miles apart." Then something strange happened; I can only describe it as a communion between us. When I take Holy Communion at church I feel nothing, with Carl Jung, after I had said those words, it's as if we merged; we melted into one. Emotionally, it was more intense than any sexual climax that I have ever experienced

27

It was December; Christmas wasn't far away. I was at the kiosk when a Jewish client gave me a Christmas present. It was a dictionary on Jewish traditions and legends by Alan Unterman. I thumbed through it and wasn't at all impressed with what was written about Jesus. I sensed that it had been given to me for a purpose but didn't know what that purpose was. Just then my husband came to replace me while I went to the shops to buy myself some lunch. I was walking down the street towards the delicatessen when I glanced into a draper's window with fitted sheets displayed, (In Italian literally angled sheets.) As I was reading "angled sheets" a voice in my head said, angels not angles. I realised that I should consult the book under angels.

That was my introduction to kabbala, up until that moment I had never heard of it. I immediately bought an anthology of cabbalistic writings and was guided towards the "Sefer Yesirah," the book of formation; tradition has it that the book was given to Abraham directly from God.

Over a period of time I was initiated into the secrets of the kabbala. God created the heavens and the earth with a compass and ruler, explained Saint Michael and I drew my own diagram of the Tree of Life following his instructions .The Tree of Life is a blue print of all the different kingdoms of God; mineral, vegetable, animal, human, angelic and cosmic. It is the origin of the Star of David. I had often asked my Jewish clients what was its origin; most were unsure, some said that it had been the symbol on the shield of king David, but now it's clear that it was much older than that and had been given to Abraham by God Himself.

Each planet is governed by an archangel: Saturn by Saint Tsafkiel, Jupiter by Saint Kamael, Mars by Saint Michael, the sun by Saint Raphael, Venus by Saint Gabriel, Mercury by Saint Tsadkiel and the moon by Saint Raziel. It is important at this point to clarify the role of these mighty archangels and what our attitude towards them should be.

The role of the archangels of the Tree of Life can be compared to the role of a government and God's role can be compared to that of a king or a queen, which rules over parliament. God alone should be worshipped; our attitude towards the archangels should be deference not adoration.

Before God created the universe, He needed a blueprint on which to trace His thoughts; kabbala is that blueprint. That is why to study kabbala, is to study God's mind, it must therefore, be approached with reverence and humility.

Throughout the ages, God has divulged His secrets to a few chosen individuals, the initiates. This is because the majority of people were not mature enough to receive them. They would have used God's secrets to enrich themselves or to wreck revenge on their enemies. Ultimately, God's secrets are being peddled for a high price by unscrupulous merchants to a few rich clients, this has to change.

I don't know why Saint Michael chose me as his spokesperson, but I am aware, not only of the privilege, but also of the grave responsibility that it pertains.

The first step Saint Michael took to introduce me to kabbala was to instruct me how to draw the tree of life. I have since seen two different versions in circulation, but they are both very different from the one which I was shown. Saint Michael then asked me to allocate the different planets and stars to it and I could hear the good humoured chuckling of the Archangels at my feeble attempts.

Archangels are wonderful gentle beings and have a distinct sense of humour. I remember once having to deliver flowers for a wedding to a country church outside of Milan. It was Sunday morning and there wasn't anyone around to ask the way, so when I realised that I was lost, nightmarish images flashed across my mind of arriving too late with the ceremony already started. I could feel myself starting to panic and prayed to Saint Michael to guide me to the right church in plenty of time to arrange the flowers. I did arrive in time and on the way back to Milan, to my surprise, I heard Saint Raphael, not Saint Michael saying, *I've done lots of things throughout the centuries but this is the first time that I have ever been asked to be a delivery boy for a florist.*

More information about kabbala is available on the website **www.stmichaelsblog.com**

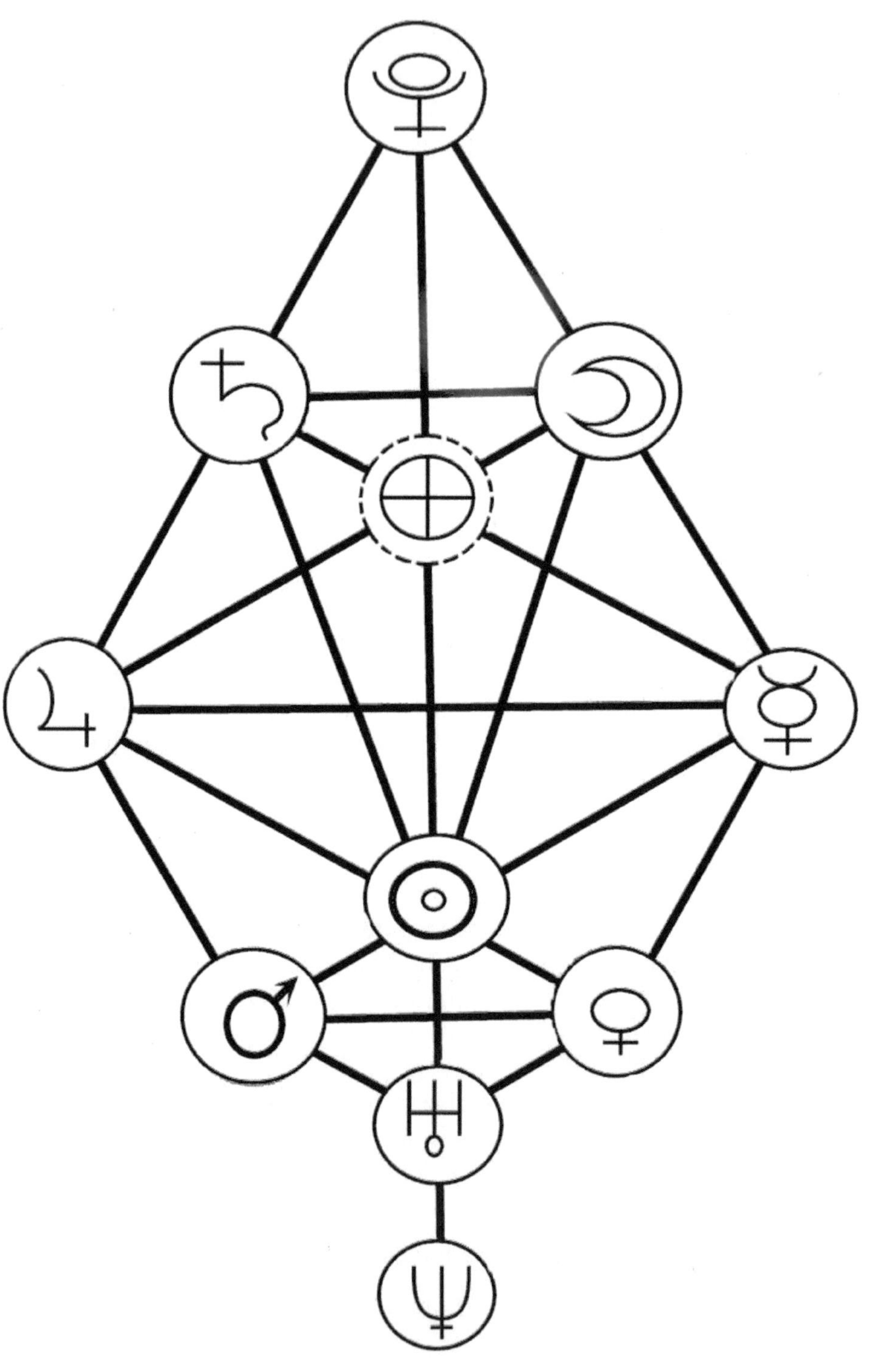

Jewish letter	In the person	In the Soul	In the year	In the cosmos
aleph	torso	equilibrium	tepid humidity	air/spirit
bet	mouth	life - death	Saturday	Saturn
gimel	right eye	peace - evil	Sunday	Jupiter
dalet	left eye	wisdom - foolishness	Monday	mars
he	liver	eyesight - blindness	Nissan	Aries
wew	bile	hearing - deafness	Iyyar	Taurus
zayin	spleen	able / unable to smell	Siwan	Gemini
het	stomach	speech - dumbness	Tammuz	cancer
tet	right kidney	nutrition - hunger	Av	Leo
yod	left kidney	action - paralysis	Elul	Virgo
kaf	right nostril	wealth - poverty	Tuesday	sun
lamed	intestine	coition - impotence	Tiari	Libra
mem	abdomen	indulgence	cold	earth/water
nun	bowel	motion - lameness	Markesan	scorpion
samek	right hand	fury - lack of liver	Kislew	Sagittarius
ayin	left hand	laughter - lack of spleen	Tevet	Capricorn
peh	left nostril	fertility - sterility	Wednesday	Venus
sade	right foot	meditation - lack of heart	Sevat	Aquarius
qof	left foot	composure - perversion	Adar	Pisces
res	right ear	grace - ugliness	Thursday	mercury
sin	head	intransigence	heat	fire/heaven
tew	left ear	sovereignty - slavery	Friday	moon

28

In my dream I was a servant in the house of God; I had no uniform; I was dressed in jeans and a t-shirt. After I had served Him supper, He asked me to go upstairs and bring His cigarettes, which were in His jacket pocket. I climbed the stairs and met two maids dressed in pink. They asked me what I wanted and after I told them they burst out laughing in disbelief. There were no cigarettes left because they had smoked them all.

Shortly afterwards I went to a Rose and Cross conference and realised that the two maids in my dream represented occult Christian groups. I interpreted that dream to mean that they were, "selling Him short." I believe that God intended religion to be organised in the same way that schools are organised, teaching the basic laws of God as preached by Moses, (primary education) followed by the teachings of the grace of God taught by Jesus, (secondary education.) In 1 Corinthians chapter 11 it is written, when I was a child I talked like a child, I thought like a child, I reasoned like a child. When I became a man I put childish things behind me. The teachings of kabbala (university) are intended for those who choose to search further for God's truth. Kabbala teachings are being sold at a high price to rich clients who can afford it and are leaving the bulk of society starving for further spiritual education. I know that God wants me to reveal these truths; the people are ready; this is the real meaning of Isaiah chapter 39.

****

I was at Holy Mass in the chapel of the cemetery, in the queue to receive Holy Communion. The woman next to me dropped the sacrament; I tried to catch it before it touched the floor but didn't succeed. I picked it up off the floor and was about to put it in my mouth when I realised that I had better give it back to the priest. He blew on it on both sides before placing it on my tongue.

Later on in the cemetery I had this vision. I was on foot following behind Saint Michael, who was riding on a white horse; behind me was a multitude of wounded men and women. Saint

Michael was leading us towards some hills that I could see in the distance. He stopped suddenly and turning around, looked past me to scrutinise the crowd. I turned also to see what he was observing and was dismayed at the scene of utter dejection. Exhausted people were following blindly, dragging their feet one after the other, carrying those that were too badly wounded to make it without help. It was similar to the scene of misery and pessimism in the film, "Gone with the Wind," when the southern army was retreating from northern troops. I exclaimed, "Oh Saint Michael, it's true that we are many, but look at us, look at our wounds, we're in no position to continue fighting." It seemed as if he were waiting for something, and at that moment the face of Jesus rose up from behind the hills in front of us, just as if it were the rising sun. He breathed on us and when his breath reached each person, it healed all of their wounds and their misery was transformed into joy.

Dare I hope that it is related to the book of Revelation chapter 6 verse 2? *I looked and there before me was a white horse! Its rider held a bow, and he was given a crown, and he rode out as a conqueror bent on conquest.*

29

I caught an infection of the gums and was told that I should have all of my teeth extracted. I decided to have a few sessions with a pranatherapist (the Italian equivalent of spiritual healer,) after all I had nothing to lose. In one of the sessions I asked him who his spirit guide was and he mumbled something about an Italian doctor.

That night as I was putting the boys to bed, I lay down beside them until they drifted off to sleep. A tall man with Negroid features appeared to me. “Who are you?” I asked. He conveyed to me that he was the spirit guide of the healer I had seen earlier in the day and asked me if I wanted a healing session. I nodded my agreement and as he healed me I scrutinised him more closely and realised that he looked more Egyptian than Negro. Halfway through the session my youngest child started to cry and while I was attending to him I saw the Egyptian in the sitting room browsing through my books. We continued the session and at the end of it he disappeared abruptly before I could even thank him. The next time that I went to my pranatherapist appointment I told him of the episode and he admitted that in fact his spirit guide was indeed an Egyptian doctor of ancient times; he apologised to me for fobbing me off with a lie

I would just like to add that during the sessions with the pranatherapist, I felt no pain whatsoever; the session with his spirit guide was very painful.

****

Early one morning, still in bed I had a vision of my sister-in-law and myself clutching each other and screaming in utter terror. We were in my sitting room standing in ankle deep water. Its walls were made of glass and as I looked out of the northeast wall, I saw a nuclear explosion mushrooming upwards. I interpreted that to mean that there would be a nuclear war starting in Germany (Germany is roughly northeast of Milan.) I started to hoard tins of food and only stopped three years later when the Chernobyl explosion occurred. I suppose I was the only person in the world to breathe a sigh of relief at that time.

I was given no prior warning to the tragedy of 9.11.01; I do know that it is linked to the book of Revelation chapter 18 verses 9 to 19.

When the kings of the earth who committed adultery with her and shared her luxury see the smoke of her burning, they will weep and mourn over her. Terrified at her torment, they will stand far off and cry:

"Woe! Woe, O great city,

O Babylon, city of power!

In one hour your doom has come!"

The merchants of the earth will weep and mourn over her because no-one buys their cargoes any more- cargoes of gold, silver, precious stones and pearls; fine linen, purple, silk and scarlet cloth; every sort of citron wood, and articles of every kind made of ivory, costly wood, bronze, iron and marble; cargoes of cinnamon and spice, myrrh and frankincense, of wine and olive oil, of fine flour and wheat; cattle and sheep; horses and carriages; and bodies and souls of men.

"They will say, 'The fruit you longed for is gone from you. All your riches and splendour have vanished, never to be recovered.' The merchants who sold these things and gained their wealth from her will stand far off, terrified at her torment. They will weep and mourn and cry out:

"Woe! Woe, O great city,

Dressed in fine linen, purple and scarlet,

And glittering with gold, precious stones and pearls!

In one hour such great wealth has been brought to ruin!'

Every sea captain and all who travel by ship, the sailors, and all who earn their living from the sea will stand far off. When they see the smoke of her burning, they will exclaim, 'Was there ever a city like this great city?' They will throw dust on their heads and with weeping and mourning cry out:

"'Woe! Woe, O great city, where all who had ships on the sea

became rich through her wealth! In one hour she has been brought to ruin.'"

I have had two other "political" visions. In the first one I saw a map of Europe slowly turning red. The red came up from northern Africa and seeped up through Italy then on into the other European countries. The only places that stayed white were the Scandinavian countries; they just had a few patches of red in them. I had always thought that this vision was announcing the migration of hundreds of thousands of people invading Europe from Africa and Eastern Europe after the fall of the Berlin Wall, but recently I'm beginning to think that it might refer to a future invasion of Europe by people from Africa escaping famine due to global warming.

The second vision happened many years later. I saw a beautiful young woman being courted by an old man. A second beautiful woman stood watching and was obviously very peeved at what she saw; she walked off in disgust.

I asked Saint Michael what the meaning was and he said that the first young woman was Russia, the second was USA and the old man was Europe.

30

I could never get my head around the concept of eternal hell. It's like throwing someone into a dungeon and throwing away the key; how could an all-loving God do that? "It must be true," I reasoned, "Because Jesus said it." On the other hand it seemed in complete contrast to his other statements; when asked by Peter how many times he should forgive his brother when he sins against him, seven times perhaps. Seventy times seven, was the reply (Matthew 18:22.) I understood this to mean always; so does God not put into practice what He preaches? I had that concept explained to me with a direct experience.

I decided to go to Benny Hinn's miracle crusade; my faith was waning and I needed my batteries recharging. It ran from Friday evening up until late Saturday evening, so I arranged to stay at a friend's house, which was near the venue, to save on expenses. I arrived in good time; I didn't have a ticket to get in because they had been sold out two months previously. There were two queues, one for ticket holders and one for none holders. I positioned myself in the none queue, expecting a long wait; the organisers were obliged to allow all of the ticket holders in first, in order to calculate how many empty seats were available for the people without tickets. I felt a tap on my shoulder, I turned around and there was this sweet old lady from Nigeria offering me a ticket. I couldn't express my gratitude enough; she had saved me hours of anxious waiting; at my age and after two heart attacks two things were to be avoided like the plague, physical exhaustion and mental stress.

We started chatting and she told me that she had nowhere to stay that night but God would provide. I immediately telephoned my friend to ask permission to take her home with me, but couldn't reach her. I did manage to speak to her son however and explained to him how I would like to return the favour of the sweet Nigerian lady; he promised to get his mother to phone me. Her call arrived fifteen minutes later and after a brief exchange, she conceded to allow my new friend to stay with me at her house for the two nights. I told my companion and she was delighted, "You see," she said, "God always provides." We spent an hour happily browsing through the CD's and books before seating ourselves. The crusade was about to begin when I received a further telephone call from my friend; she was furious. She accused me of deceiving her; I had not mentioned to her that my friend was black. I assured her that it had not been intentional; it had not occurred to me that the colour of my friend's skin might be an issue. I later learned that her son had met her at the pub and on hearing that his mother had allowed my friend into her home; he had laughingly accused her of changing her tune. I had not known that my friend was racist; I hadn't even realised that I had omitted that information in our brief telephone conversation. I was very embarrassed; I didn't know what to do. I decided not to say anything to my new friend until the end of the evening; I didn't want to spoil her night, mine was already spoilt. I eventually mumbled something about my friend's daughter turning up at her mother's house without warning so there was no room for either of us; we eventually found a cheap B&B nearby.

That episode ruined my weekend; it wouldn't leave my mind; how could a nice, amiable, generous person like my friend be so prejudiced?

On the train back home I started to pray to Saint Michael. "Please intercede for my friend to God our Father," I implored, "Please don't let her be hurled into eternal hell, please save her." Saint Michael replied by explaining to me that God our Father is 100% love and truth; He does not allocate anybody anywhere; we do it all ourselves. When people leave their physical bodies they see a "Film" of their lives just passed on earth and re-live all of the hurt they have inflicted on others. They are then summoned in front of the throne of God and usually kneel shaking with apprehension knowing that they fell short of the expectations set for them on earth. Eventually they pick up enough courage to peek at the face of God and it is then that their fate is sealed. *God assumes the appearance of your worst enemy*, Saint Michael explained. "Oh," I exclaimed, "So in the case of my friend God will appear black and point His finger at her and rebuke her just as she rebuked black people in her life and banish her to hell forever and ever?" *No, no, no,* said Saint Michael, *You have got it all wrong. How can a loving father do such a thing to his adored child? At that moment, He opens His arms and invites His child to clamber up to be embraced. It is His child that recoils from His caresses, just as your friend recoils from black people here on earth, so she will instinctively recoil from the presence of a black God after her death.*

"Wow," I thought, "Whose face will God assume in my case?" When the time comes, I wonder what Gerry Adam's reaction will be when he looks up into a blown-up version of Ian Paisley, or visa versa, what will Reverend Paisley do when a blown-up version of Mr. Adams opens his arms and invites him up for a cuddle?

31

I find it very difficult to have orderly and coherent thoughts about creation. As a Christian, I would like to believe in the six-day creation story in the Genesis, but my logical brain prevents me from doing so. Let there be light, pronounced by God on the first day of creation, cannot refer to sunlight because the sun was not created until the fourth day. Is it possible that those poetic words of God and Stephen Hawkin's understatement of "The Big Bang," are both referring to the same occurrence?

I asked Saint Metatron for knowledge; he guided me to a sequence of lectures by a Rose and Cross group. I wasn't impressed but I persevered until the end because I knew that I had been sent for a purpose. Before the very last lecture, someone gave me a book, "I Misteri dell'Opera Divina," which helped me to put together all of the disjointed pieces of information that I had scattered around my mind regarding creation.

The entity that we know as God is the creator of our universe. He is composed of all of the relative love and all of the relative truth of every person through the ages in the creation before ours; together they form absolute love and absolute truth.

There exists however another God, the Supreme Being who is responsible for all of the Gods, the creators of all of the different universes in all of creation.

Our solar system became manifest with the big bang and will end when our sun dies. That period is divided into seven different manifestations; we are now living in the fourth manifestation. The twelve zodiac signs delimit the space in which the manifestation occupies.

In the beginning, it's as if sparks were emitted from God; we are those sparks; virgin spirits, blank pages upon which the story of evolution is being written, our physical, emotional, intellectual and spiritual evolution. The first cosmic day can be described as the mineral manifestation, I was a tiny speck of sand then, as were most of us; our physical bodies originate from that manifestation which lasted millions of years. It was followed by the first cosmic night when God assimilated all of the experiences of that day.

The minerals that adjusted to the changing environment were reincarnated as members of the vegetable kingdom and the second cosmic day was born. Those that didn't adjust remained in the mineral kingdom as swamps and mobile sands together with the new virgin spirits emitted from God. We acquired our ethereal (mental) bodies from that manifestation, which lasted millions of years. It was followed by the second cosmic night when God assimilated all of the experiences of the second day.

The third cosmic day saw all of the vegetable kingdom that had adjusted to the changes appearing as members of the animal kingdom; among other things I was an orang-utan in that manifestation; those that didn't adjust remained as carnivorous plants and insects. We acquired our emotional or astral bodies from that manifestation which lasted millions of years. It was followed by the third cosmic night when God assimilated all of the experiences of that day.

The fourth (present) cosmic day was announced by the appearance of human beings, the reincarnation of all of the different animals that had adjusted successfully to the changing environment. Up to now, in this manifestation I have been incarnated as Jacob, Saul, Mary Magdalene, an Indian squaw and myself. It is in this manifestation that we acquire our Ego or will power; we choose to grow in love and truth or choose not to. Those animals that did not have the ability to adjust remained in the animal kingdom as bears and primates. When this manifestation ends, the fourth cosmic night will appear and God will assimilate all of the experiences of the fourth day.

The fifth cosmic day will see us as angels, assisting the new human beings that will reincarnate from the present day animals. Those of us that did not adjust (grow sufficiently in love and truth) will remain in this dimension as earthbound spirits. In the fifth cosmic night God will assimilate all of the experiences of all of the beings in the angelic realm from the humblest of fairies to the mightiest of Archangels.

By the end of the fifth cosmic day, every one of us that has been able to adjust to the changing environment will enter into the sixth cosmic day which is the cosmic kingdom; we will influence positively, decisions made by individuals here on earth. Those that cannot adjust will remain in the angelic kingdom as demons, (fallen angels.) I know nothing about the sixth cosmic day except that it prepares us to become part of the body of a new God and we will then be ready to manifest our own creative powers in the next creation. Our present God will move on to greater things. What a privilege it will be for those of us evolved enough to be part of a new God-body composed of the positive energies of people like Jesus, Moses, Gandhi, Buddha, Mohamed, the Dalai Lama, Saint Francis, mother Theresa, Nelson Mandela, Pope John II, Karl Marx and all of the more ordinary men and women who have cultivated within themselves unconditional love for others and found some of God's truth.

More information about creation is available on the website **www.stmichaelsblog.com.**

32

When I was living in Italy, I used to attend church every day. Here in England, that wasn't possible so when I heard of the possibility of attending an Evangelical group, I jumped at the chance; it filled a need in me to praise God with songs and spontaneous prayer, but it was too radical for my liking. After a few weeks I had this dream.

I was in a house with two rooms. I knocked on one of the doors and my mother answered it; I looked beyond her and could see my sister sitting on the sofa. "Go away," my mother barked at me, "Can't you see that we're watching a video? Go and join your brothers and sisters in the next room;" she slammed the door in my face. I went into the next room, which was complete bedlam. There were children of all ages doing exactly as they liked with no supervision whatsoever. The television was blasting out its programmes and nobody seemed to be watching it. Younger children were crying and appeared neglected; older ones were laughing and seemed as if they were having a whale of a time whilst others cried silently. "I can't stand this mess," I said and started to look for my shoes, which I had taken off at the entrance of the house. There was a big pile of them in the corner and I started to rummage through it. Not being able to find the shoes that I had come in, I eventually found a black patent leather one, which fitted my left foot perfectly. I continued looking for its mate but to no avail; I made do with a black cloth slipper to put on my right foot, which was much too small for me; I pulled down the heel and wore it as a flip-flop.

On analysing the dream, I've come to the conclusion that the left patent leather shoe represents my catholic faith; perfect fit, but incomplete. The black slipper which I put on my right foot is the Evangelical group that I am attending; comfortable for two thirds, but far two small for me. My mother and sister represented people who do not follow any organised religion; the children in the next room represented all of the different evangelical churches that exist.

I started to ask myself what was missing in my catholic faith and I've decided that my religion can be divided into two parts. The first is the necessity I feel to worship God. Not everyone feels this urge and I can empathise with those that don't, because that is where I came from. The second part is learning about God's truth, God's laws; this is the part that I find lacking and no amount of church attendance or group meetings can fill this void. Thank God that Saint Michael came to my rescue with kabbala teachings and these modern day parables to teach me how to live my faith.

****

An Evangelist once criticised me for collecting stones and gems, according to her it was from the devil. I didn't argue with her but when I got home I asked Saint Michael if it were true. *Is poetry bad?* Was the reply? *Just as flowers are the visual poetry of the vegetable kingdom, so gems are the visual poetry of the mineral kingdom. To be able to appreciate a poem, you must at least be able to understand the language it is written in, but no intellect is necessary to be touched by the beauty of a flower or a gem.*

Some one else criticised me for my love of jazz; "The devil's music," was the cry. I didn't even bother checking that one out.

33

A few months have past and I'm finding the Evangelical group heavy going; I am convinced that I have nothing in common with them. I can feel the animosity as soon as I walk into the room. It's not only because I am a practicing catholic, believe in reincarnation and practice kabbala but because I respect other religions and believe that even atheists go to heaven (sixth astral plane); worst of all, I do not believe that the world was created in six days. As far as they are concerned I am guilty of, "intellectual arrogance." After the umpteenth time of trying to reconcile my views with theirs and failing miserably, I decided to call it a day. "That's it," I said out loud to Saint Michael, "I'm not going back; I can't see the point in prolonging the agony any longer." About half an hour later I heard Saint Michael's reply. *It is true that the contents of your mind are very different from the contents of Silvia's. You have both lived on different continents, in different cities and have been influenced by different cultures. It is also true that the love that Silvia has in her heart for God is just as fervent as the love that you have in your heart for Him; so instead of erecting a dividing wall between the contents of your minds, would it not be better to build a church using the contents of both your hearts as a sound foundation?*

I have decided to continue attending the twice-weekly meetings but it's not getting any easier.

In one of the Evangelical meetings a video was shown which underlined the difficulties women pastors had to overcome in the past. Most of their problems were caused by prejudiced men; their own husbands played a major role in their problems. After the meeting there was a discussion, which in my opinion, turned into an excessive criticism of men in general. I left the meeting wondering why some women were so aggressive towards them, and why they had such a distorted viewpoint.

That night I dreamt that I was at a friend's farm in the south of England with a girlfriend. We decided to leave, so we both kissed my friend goodbye and started off across the field. We were half way across it when we saw a pride of lions coming towards us. I ran back from whence we had come but I saw my friend being mauled by the lions. I watched as she escaped and make it to the gate at the far end of the field. I started to run round the perimeter of the field to ascertain if she had been harmed when I came to the guardhouse. I rushed in and told the guards what had happened, their response was, "That's nothing, last night a group of seven men tried to cross the field, whilst six of them were badly injured but escaped with their lives, the seventh was completely devoured by them, the only thing we found of him was his penis."

I was puzzled over the meaning of the dream but later realised that the pride of lions represented the women of the Evangelical group; the man that was devoured was one of their husbands; the only area, which was not criticised that night and therefore acceptable was his sexual performance. That dream cheered me up no end; I think I continued laughing for at least a week. No one can tell me that angels do not have a sense of humour!

A few more months have passed and I'm still having problems with the Evangelical group that I am frequenting. Their discomfort is palpable every time I mention Saint Michael. Matters have come to a head and they have admitted that they are convinced that it is not Saint Michael the archangel that I am in contact with, but a demon. They asked me to allow them to pray over me in tongues to cast it out and I agreed. I knew that I had no demon inside of me. It is written in the bible; *by their fruits you shall recognise them. (Matthew 7:16.)* Why would a demon teach me about God's love? After a long session of praying in tongues, when nothing happened, they had to admit defeat and give up, but I'm sure that in their hearts they are still convinced that I am possessed.

I went home after that meeting with mixed feelings; sadness because they are so narrow minded that anything that they have not experienced personally, or that accepted members of their community have not experienced, is according to them of the devil. Astonishment at their arrogance, do they really want to mould everyone into being carbon copies of themselves? Anger, how dare they preach to me about being non-judgemental when they themselves have acted as judge, jury and executioner towards me? They pretend to love Jesus, but are they not acting exactly the same as the Pharisees in Jesus' time? Just as the Pharisees condemned the teachings of Jesus because they were too big to fit inside the narrow box of interpretation that they had assigned God's laws to; so these people condemn any teachings that do not fit into their own narrow interpretation of the bible. God's teachings through Jesus are so universal, that they can be embraced not only by Christians, but also by any person of another faith or of no faith at all. The biggest fault with Christianity as far as I am concerned, is that all of the emphasise has and is being put on the messenger and not enough on the content of the message. Yes, I believe that Jesus is the second person of the trinity, yes it is right for Christians to worship him, but do not condemn atheists or people of other faiths who live his teachings of love and tolerance every day of their lives, without accepting him as God.

What really annoyed the group was when I told them of Saint Michael's reply to me after I had asked him to suggest an historic Christian other than Jesus on whom I could model my Christianity (see chapter 11),his reply, "Mahatma Ghandi," did not enthral them. According to them, a Christian can be defined as such when they accept Jesus as their saviour and lord, never mind their behaviour and they have many quotes from scripture to back them up.

My stance is different; I believe that a Christian can be defined by his behaviour. I base this belief on Saint Michael's teaching (see chapter 11,) on Jesus' teaching (see chapter 11) and on the numerous quotations from scripture:

(James 2:26,) *as the body without the spirit is dead, so faith without deeds is dead.*

(Matthew 7:21-28,) *Not everyone who says to me, 'Lord, Lord,' will enter into the kingdom of heaven, but only he who does the will of my Father who is in heaven. Many will say to me on that day, 'Lord, Lord, did we not prophesy in your name and in your name drive out demons and perform many miracles?' Then I will tell them plainly, 'I never knew you. Away from me you evil doers.'*

(Matthew 12:50,) *for whoever does the will of my Father in heaven is my brother and sister and mother.*

(Matthew 16:27) *For the Son of Man is going to come in his Father's glory with his angels, and then he will reward each person according to what he has done.*

(Luke 6:46-49) *why do you call me Lord, Lord, and do not do as I say? I will show you what he is like who comes to me and hears my words and puts them into practice. He is like a man building a house, who dug down deep and laid the foundation on rock. When the flood came, the torrent struck that house but could not shake it, because it was well built. But the one who hears my words and does not put them into practice is like a man who built a house on the ground without a foundation. The moment the torrent struck that house, it collapsed and its destruction was complete.*

And the daddy of them all, (Matthew 25:31-46) *When the Son of Man comes in his glory, and all the angels with him, he will sit on his throne in heavenly glory. All the nations will be gathered before him, and he will separate the people one from another as a shepherd separates the sheep from the goats. He will put the sheep on his right and the goats on his left.*

Then the king will say to those on his right, 'Come, you who are blessed by my father; take your inheritance, the kingdom prepared for you since the creation of the world. For I was hungry and you gave me something to eat, I was thirsty and you gave me something to drink. I was a stranger and you invited me in, I needed clothes and you clothed me, I was sick and you looked after me, I was in prison and you came to visit me.

Then the righteous will answer him, 'Lord, when did we see you hungry and feed you, or thirsty and give you something to drink? When did we see you a stranger and invite you in, or needing clothes and clothed you? When did we see you sick or in prison and go to visit you?'

The King will reply, 'I tell you the truth, whatever you did for one of the least of these brothers of mine, you did for me.'

Then he will say to those on his left, 'Depart from me, you who are cursed, into the eternal fire prepared for the devil and his angels. For I was hungry and you gave me nothing to eat, I was thirsty and you gave me nothing to drink, I was a stranger and you did not invite me in, I needed clothes and you did not clothe me, I was sick and in prison and you did not look after me.'

They also will answer, 'Lord, when did we see you hungry or thirsty or a stranger or needing clothes or sick or in prison, and did not help you?'

He will reply, 'I tell you the truth, whatever you did not do for one of the least of these, you did not do for me.'

Then they will go away to eternal punishment, but the righteous to eternal life.

I am absolutely convinced that the mission of every person on this earth is to fill their hearts with love and their minds with truth. What determines our spiritual evolution is the amount of love and kindness we express to others. That means that I believe wholeheartedly that heaven, (the sixth astral plane) is full of loving people, loving Jews, loving Moslems, loving Hindus, loving Buddhists, loving atheists as well as loving Christians. They are there because they have put into practice in their daily lives Matthew 25: 31-46 consciously or unconsciously, not because of lip service to Jesus, or Buddha or Mohamed or Moses or anyone else.

Jesus was in constant fellowship with God. At any time of the day or night he had access to his father. His words "*My God, my God, why have you forsaken me?*"(Matthew 27:46) when he was on the cross used to puzzle me; surely the only time that Jesus had real need of his father was then. The explanation I was given was that sin separates us from God. Adam and Eve, the moment they sinned, automatically excluded themselves from the fellowship they had with God (Genesis 3:8-9.*Then the man and his wife heard the sound of the Lord God as he was walking in the garden in the cool of the day, and they hid from the Lord God among the trees of the garden.*) Jesus took upon himself all of the sins of humanity when he was nailed to the cross. The physical pain must have been unbearable, but what distressed him most was the consequence of sin, being separated from his father. Even though the sin was not his, he was still obliged to succumb to God's law.

I asked Saint Michael why, if Jesus had taken our sins from us when he was on the cross, was the karmic law still in force. He told me to think of it as the cancellation of debt. Even when poor nations have their national debt cancelled, each individual still has a long way to go before becoming rich.

****

In my dream I was walking down a street and saw on the opposite pavement a woman pastor with a lovely, long, thick plait. I expressed my admiration of it to the person at my side who replied, "It's false." "Don't be silly," I said, "It can't be false." At that moment the woman pulled off her hat together with her plait before entering her home.

I believe that that was Saint Michael's way of telling me that not every Pastor was genuinely sent by God; some were convinced that they were, but in actual fact were being deceived by the devil.

In my dream I walked up to a very ancient oak tree; its trunk was so vast that five men holding hands would have had difficulty in embracing it. From behind it a John-the Baptist-like figure emerged; he was naked except for an animal skin around his loins. "Who are you?" I asked. "Isaiah," he replied. He then stooped down and from a hole in the base of the trunk extracted something. He gave it to me and disappeared. I looked down at what he had given me; it was a modern day plastic freezer bag containing dried meat.

****

I discovered my name written eight times in the Italian translation of the New Jerusalem Bible, four times in the book of Isaiah chapter 28 verse 10,

Precetto su precetto, precetto su precetto,

norma su norma, norma su norma,

un po' qui, un po'la.

And repeated in verse 13,

Precetto su precetto, precetto su precetto,

norma su norma, norma su norma,

un po' qui, un po' la.

The English translation according to the NIV Bible is;

Do and do, do and do,

Rule on rule, rule on rule,

A little here, a little there.

Isaiah was preaching to a mocking audience against drunken priests and false prophets. I often wonder on the significance it might have.

****

35

It was in the early sixties; I was in my teens and still a virgin. I'd left home after a row with my father and was staying with an aunt. Her house was very modest; there was no bathroom and the toilet was outside in the yard. I decided to take a bath; everyone had gone out for the night and I was alone. I prepared the tin bath in front of the fire, filled it with water, undressed and stepped in. I bent down to pick up the soap and at that moment the dog licked me once on my most intimate part. I've always felt guilty about the sheer pleasure that rippled up and down my spine instead of the disgust that I ought to have felt. I take comfort in the words of psalm 25:7, *"Remember not the sins of my youth and my rebellious ways."*

****

I decided to go to confession; I had quite a few sins to confess so as soon as I had knelt down in the confessional and the preliminaries were played out, I started to confess my sins. I was immediately interrupted by the priest, who started to lecture me on how the blouse I was wearing was not modest enough; it was sleeveless, high necked but sleeveless. I offered my apologies and started again on my long list of sins that I had prepared before hand. He interrupted me again for the same reason. I again apologised and attempted for the third time to continue my confession when he again interrupted me and gave me a long lecture on inappropriate dress in church. He eventually gave me the absolution for inappropriate dress but had not even given me the chance to confess my sins.

As I was reciting my penance afterwards in the church, he walked passed me and I started to ask myself why he had put so much emphasis on the outward correctness and given no time at all to what I considered real sins. I immediately had this vision. The surrounding church disappeared and I was on a flat roof somewhere in Egypt; I could see the pyramids in the distance. I was watching a function, taking place in honour of the sun god. The priest that had just walked by was the officiator at the ceremony.

A Buddhist friend of mine once invited me to a Buddhist prayer meeting. We were slightly late and it had already started when we arrived. We took off our shoes and knelt down at the back of the room where mantras were being chanted. After about ten minutes my head started spinning and I felt sick. I somehow found the bathroom but passed out before I could get to the toilet. I woke up lying on the bathroom floor in a pool of my own vomit.

36

One day my husband asked me to deposit some money at the bank on the other side of the square where the shop was. Walking just ahead of me was a very attractive young woman who lived in the same building; she was a high-class prostitute. She was stunning and as I was walking behind her I could see the reaction of the people that were walking towards her. Some of the men were very noisy in their appraisal, even stopping after she had passed them to admire her from behind; my presence went unnoticed. She didn't have to wait to cross over the road because as soon as the policeman saw her he obligingly stopped the traffic; I hurried after her, grateful for not having to waste the usual five or six minutes before crossing. As she neared the doors of the bank, they opened as if by magic; she pranced in not even acknowledging the presence of the man who had held the doors open for her. I thanked him but he was too busy admiring her bum to hear me.

I took my place in the queue after her so had a front row view of the clerk that was serving her. Was it really that same middle-aged man that had a beer belly and suffered from arthritis? He seemed years younger and was even witty in his banter. She deposited the same amount of money that I was depositing; hers was tax-free. Once our overheads were deducted, taxes paid and suppliers satisfied, I wondered how much remained ours. His eyes followed her wistfully as she swept majestically out of the bank; he didn't even respond to my greeting.

Coming out of the bank I could see her ahead of me and by the time that I had crossed over the road, she had already disappeared into the courtyard and past by the back door of the shop. The straw that really broke the camel's back was seeing the expression on my husband's face as he gazed longingly towards the lift that had just whisked her away, her perfume still lingering in the air.

That did it! I made an excuse and went home to lick my wounds. "I've done everything wrong," I mused to myself. "I was pretty when I was young; I had the opportunity of being admired and pampered and courted by men; I turned down a few proposals which would have feathered my nest. Instead, here I am 40 years old looking 50; too tired after a hard days work to even finish the weekly ironing, having no time nor inclination to look after myself; I put the needs of my three kids and my husband before my own and what thanks do I get? Nothing, I'm not even appreciated."

Later on Saint Michael came through. *Think of yourself and that young lady as two lions,* he said, *proudly stalking the savannahs of Africa. One day however, she was captured by men and taken to a zoo. Yes, she has someone to clean out her cage for her; someone else brings her food and if she becomes sick she is lovingly nursed back to health by dedicated vets and yes, she will probably live longer than you. You on the other hand are still in the wild, hunting with the pack to feed your cubs; your mane is mangy, you have been wounded many times and each day is a battle for survival. But if only you could see yourself from my perspective, you would have no doubts about having made the right decision. Your dignity shines out like a beacon; instead of feeling envy for her, you should be feeling pity.*

That pep talk perked me up no end; I even made my husband his favourite meal.

37

It seemed that every time I went to press the button of the lift it was out of order, that meant walking up three flights of stairs. I was six months pregnant with my second child and Patrick; my first child was about a year old and very heavy, so it must have been in 1976. After three days I was at the end of my tether and complained to my husband. “That’s strange,” he replied, “The lift’s working alright for me, how about you dad?” It turned out that my father-in-law had had an argument with the caretaker and had not given her the tip that she was accustomed to receiving at that time of year. Not being able to wreak her revenge on him, (He uses the lift only very early in the mornings and late at night before and after she started and finished work,) she turned her attention to me, the weakest link; when she saw me going towards the lift laden with groceries, she would turn it off.

I felt sick to my stomach, how could anyone be so cruel? I was furious, I stopped talking to her, I would cross over the road to avoid her if I saw her coming towards me; I felt repugnance when she was near me. This situation continued for years, until my encounter with Saint Michael after the birth of my third child. I realised that I had to forgive her, easier said than done; I couldn’t bring myself to do it. I compromised; I used to pray to God to give me the ability to forgive her. Months passed then one day, quite out of the blue she came up to me and started to tell me her life story. I was amazed; we hadn’t even said bongiorno to each other for years and here she was, telling me very personal details of her life. As her story unfolded, I realised that her behaviour was only the product of her instinct for survival. I could feel the animosity that I felt towards her slowly melting; pity took its place and eventually I was able to forgive her.

Why can’t the same thing happen with my mother? Armed with that experience of over thirty years ago, why can’t I apply it to the present situation and eliminate the resentment that I feel towards her. Why was I able to forgive a complete stranger and not a close relative whom I love?

Last week I saw her in a dream, the first time in years. I was sitting watching television when I heard the front door opening. I went to investigate and saw my mother and father tiptoeing upstairs. I started shouting at her and calling her names; she started to cry and the dream ended with us both half-heartedly throwing things at each other.

Yet I have no problem in forgiving David, my son. As Jacob, I created all of the jealously that would return to me as Saul. In that life, I as Saul banished David; (1 Samuel 19:9-10) *But an evil spirit from the Lord came upon Saul as he was sitting in his house with his spear in his hand. While David was playing the harp, Saul tried to pin him to the wall with his spear, but David eluded him as Saul drove the spear into the wall. That night David made good his escape.* In my present life, David is responsible for my "banishment" but I can honestly say that I feel no resentment or animosity towards him whatsoever.

Mario, my spiritual son is HIV positive and years ago, after praying for his healing, Saint Michael promised that if I forgave my mother, he would heal Mario. I went to Findhorn especially for that purpose but Mario wasn't healed; I can only conclude that I failed miserably to forgive her. I have decided to make another attempt and so I asked for inner healing from the Evangelical group I am attending. Before the meeting took place, I prepared myself by listening to a tape given to me by the group. It was the testimony of a man who had overcome the difficult relationship that he had had with his father. I followed the advice on the tape by writing a letter to both my mother and my father. Because they had both died years before, I was unable to talk to them face to face.

Dear Dad,

I remember dedicating a pilgrimage to Our Lady to you about 20 years ago. At that time I forgave you for all of the neglect and deprivation that I had suffered. I was convinced that I had succeeded in forgiving you, so when one of the members of the Evangelical group came over to me and whispered in my ear that it had been revealed to her that I had issues with you to confront, I didn't hesitate to deny it. How wrong I was. That night, I was awoken abruptly by some of the unpleasant episodes of my childhood, which had seeped through from my unconscious to my conscious mind.

That time you stole my watch, a present from nana and granda for my ninth birthday, and gave it to your girlfriend. The Christmas Eve, when you ate the whole chicken that I had so lovingly helped mam to prepare a few hours before, ready for next day's Christmas lunch. We ate chicken soup that year, made from the bones you left. I can still see mam, the tears rolling down her face as she gathered up your leftovers and put them in a pan. All of the nights spent in walking the streets, killing time waiting for you to fall into a drunken stupor so that we could return to our beds and continue our rest before getting up for school the next day; the enforced poverty because you drank the little money that came into the house; the humiliation of wearing the cast offs from my older cousin. All of the Christmases that I received the same doll which disappeared around November miraculously reappearing on Christmas morning with different coloured eyes, a new nose and a different coloured wig, dressed in knitted clothes that I had pretended not to see being made by Auntie Jenny. We didn't even have a radio never mind a television set and I was kept in touch with teenage music by the chatter of my friends.

Yet I have no problem in forgiving you. If I'm honest, I can't say that I feel daughterly love for you, but I've always felt compassion for you ever since I was told that you were badly treated as a child at the hands of your stepmother. How could you as a parent, give to your child the love and nurture that you had not received from your parents? But my compassion for you is not enough. The question asked on the tape, "Whose daughter are you?" cries out to be answered. I am your daughter and I ask your forgiveness for all of the love that I should have given to you but did not; all of the respect that I should have given to you but did not; all of the time that I should have dedicated to you when you were dying of cancer and did not. Please can you forgive me?

Dear Mam,

"I've been listening to a tape on daughter-ship;" lots of things in the tape I can relate to; I expect you can as well; I can sense that you are here listening to it with me. What went wrong between us? When did we start disliking each other? I can't remember ever being kissed or hugged by you, why not? Was it so difficult for you to put your arms around me and convey warmth, tenderness or motherly love? I can remember trying to hug you once in Italy; there was a huge storm and I knew that you were frightened of thunder and lightning; you shrugged me off, why?

I don't know if you were reacting to my coldness or if I were reacting to yours. I do know that I'm sick and tired of trying to analyse our relationship and instead, I want to try and rectify things even if we're not together anymore. I know that I want to forgive you for not being the mother I needed; I also want to ask your forgiveness for not being the daughter you would have liked.

After your death, I remember you saying to me that you were around me because you were learning to love me; did you succeed? I'm sorry that I was so rude to you; can you forgive me?

Today I'm having a healing session with the group, I am hoping with all of my heart to be able to change my emotions towards you and dad.

"Whose daughter are you?" Until I answer that question and resolve this issue, I know that I'll not be able to continue forward on my spiritual journey. It's as if I've been putting it off for so long, always saving this issue for later, never comfortable when confronted with it. Now I must answer it; I can't put it off any longer.

Whose daughter are you? I want to be your daughter. Please forgive me for my cold arrogance, which started in my teens and has continued up to the present day. Please forgive me for being your judge, your jury and your prosecutor all rolled into one. I want to thank you for all of the sacrifices you underwent to meet all of my material needs and I realise that you had so many grave problems with dad while I was growing up, that it was impossible for you to meet my then emotional needs. I also realise that being a child with nine siblings, you probably didn't receive many cuddles from your own parents; what you don't receive, you can't pass on. Can we be friends? I know that Saint Michael will convey your answer to me sooner or later. I'm sorry I threw things at you the other night and made you cry can you forgive me?

The healing session was very painful for me and I cried buckets, but this time I really believe that I might have succeeded in forgiving her. I prayed to God and asked him to convey to me if she had forgiven me and the next night in a dream I was told yes, she had. I asked for further confirmation the next day and at random opened the bible at the book of Hosea chapter three, Hosea's reconciliation with his wife. Every day I reiterate my forgiveness for her and I'm waiting for a telephone call from Mario telling me that he is healed; it hasn't arrived yet.

39

When Bengy was small, if anything was disagreeable to him he used to call it blue. Any food he didn't like was blue; people he didn't like were blue; clothes he didn't want to wear were blue.

He was misbehaving one day, so in no uncertain terms I'd banished him kicking and screaming to his room and left him there. I returned to the kitchen and was busy washing the dishes when I heard a voice in my ear saying, "You are blue." I can only presume that it was his guardian angel chastising me for being too harsh on him.

****

One of the first visions I had after Bengy was born was seeing myself at a stall in a marketplace with absolutely nothing to sell; completely bare boards. On reflection I came to the conclusion that was exactly my state; I had nothing to offer anyone; I wasn't beautiful, or intelligent, or creative, or funny, or.... nothing. That depressed me but later I was told that it was an advantage spiritually; I had nothing to be proud about.

****

It was just before the 2nd November; I was working long hours in the cemetery; the day of the dead is an important Holy day in Italy when everyone pays a visit to their loved one's graves. There was much fervour with everyone wanting their family tombs to be cleaned and decorated with fresh flowers for the occasion.

I was busy attending to the tomb of one of my clients when I heard someone crying behind me. I turned around to see who it was but no one was there. I continued my work but the crying continued; I closed my eyes to concentrate better and heard the voice of a well known Italian celebrity lamenting the fact that no one was attending to his grave. In life this person had been part of the jet set, famous for his wild life style. I finished what I was doing then went to his grave and put some flowers on it.

Later that day at Holy Mass in the chapel of the cemetery he appeared to me and thanked me; his eyelids were sewn down so that he was unable to see.

****

I left my husband after 31 years of marriage. Two of my three children had become punks and turned my house into a squat. Complaints to my husband were of no avail, his stance was to grin and bear it. Getting no support from my husband, I turned to the church for advice, "Prayer, prayer and more prayer," was the cry. I left home on at least three occasions but always returned. The definite decision to leave for good was taken after I had just finished a meditation session; I was in my car returning home when I heard a voice saying, *we are of the opinion that if they (my sons) do not accept your teachings, then it is better to leave.* This was a response to my mental turmoil; I was unhappy, but as it is written in the bible (Ephesians 5:22*) wives submit to your husband…* I was reluctant to leave for good.

The decision was taken out of my hands at Christmas 1999; I received a telephone call from my brother telling me that my mother was dying. I caught a plane on Christmas Eve but she died while I was at Heathrow airport trying to catch a plane up north.

I never went back to Italy to live; I suppose that I did a Shirley Valentine in reverse.

****

I have always asked Saint Michael to keep me free from error. Saint Michael is the angel of wisdom in kabbala. Every day I ask in my prayers the ability to discern between God's truth and the lies of the devil; it's not always clean cut.

One day I was pondering over in my mind the notion that the Christ had entered the body of Jesus at his baptism. I had read that an early Christian sect believed that; Rudolf Steiner did as well (Background to the Gospel of St Mark-lecture 6, page 112.) The next morning, very early while I was still in bed Jesus told me that the Christ was incarnated at his birth. At his baptism He had received the Holy Spirit.

****

God the father is thought; God the son is word; God the Holy Spirit is action.

41

Because of Dan Brown's book, The Da Vinci Code, many people are speculating on whether Jesus was married or not.

At the beginning of the 1980's I met a wonderful man who became my spiritual director. He was not a priest; he had been a Franciscan monk with Padre Pio but had subsequently left the order, married and was the proud father of two children.

I used to see him every Thursday lunchtime for an hour or so and pour out to him all my troubles. Initially, our relationship was like that of a patient and her psychiatrist, but that soon changed after he told me that he loved me passionately, but without any sexual desire towards me whatsoever. I used to feel uncomfortable when he used to embrace me; I must emphasise that nothing sexual occurred or was implied at these times. It was the first and only time that I have been the object of unconditional love and didn't really understand it or believe that it existed until many years later when I felt unconditional love towards Mario, (my spiritual son.) It really is like being in love; everything is that much more intense, colours, tastes even humdrum everyday situations were exciting.

There are many different kinds of love; the love of a child for his father, the love of a mother for her child, platonic love in a friendship, the passionate love between lovers but until I experienced unconditional love personally, at first hand, I never really understood the term, "unconditional love."

This is the type of love that God feels for each of His children. Angels feel it and I am convinced that that was the type of love that Jesus felt for Mary Magdalene, every one of his disciples including Judah and each and every member of the human race, whether they accept him as God or not.

42

Last night Saint Michael scolded me in a dream. I was a clerk in an office and kept skiving. I was living with a family whose two daughters both gave birth to their children on the same night. I gave that as an excuse for going late to the office the next morning. My boss would have none of it and told me to get a move on or else. He threw a batch of new work on my desk even though I had not finished the first lot.

A few days later browsing through a second hand bookshop, I came across six or seven Rudolf Steiner books. I knew that it was connected with the dream so offered £50 for the whole lot, (In Italy, Saint Michael had often taught me concepts using Rudolf Steiner books.) My offer was accepted and I eagerly took them home to study. Sure enough, the teachings in two of the books when applied to the kabbala tree of life, fitted perfectly, forming three elegant patterns, one for the mental body, one for the emotional body and one for the spiritual body.

I often wonder why I am being taught kabbala truths, have they any practical function? Did Jesus use kabbala to heal? It sometimes feels as if I have been given a computer (the diagram of the tree of life,) the software, (The correct positioning of each Jewish letter,) but I haven't yet been taught which keys to press.

43

I've come to the "what if" stage in this enterprise. What if people don't believe me, what if somebody is offended by what I've written, what if it doesn't get published, what if?...

I've been led to the book of Jonah. I empathise with Jonah, he didn't want to go to Nineveh to preach and I didn't want to divulge my experiences. He eventually went and preached and they believed him and one hundred and twenty thousand people were saved. I don't presume to influence so many people but it would be nice to think that this book might make a few people ponder over their own life philosophy. 5000 years ago Moses introduced humanity to God's justice; 2000 years ago Jesus introduced us to God's love; the present time has been chosen for Saint Michael to introduce us to God's truth, which is:

- Each person's guardian angel is waiting for him or her to evolve enough to start an individual fellowship with them and lead them back to God.
- It takes more than one lifetime to attain perfection hence reincarnation.
- Obedience to God's laws means union with God; disobedience means separation.
- To be defined as a Christian means putting into practice the teachings of Jesus, not just worshipping him. This means that all peoples of different faiths, and those without faith, are eligible.
- It is important to free our senses of all addictions thus liberating our spirit.
- Every individual is personally responsible for his or her own spiritual evolvement; it cannot be delegated to a church.
- God exists; He is the personification of absolute love and absolute truth.
- Satan exists; He is the personification of evil and ignorance, (the absence of love and truth.)

Nobody has 100% of truth. The amount of truth contained in a person is in direct proportion to the amount of love contained in that person. My imperfections are apparent to everyone close to me therefore I suggest that you accept that which you can and leave the rest. We are all at different levels of evolvement, if your personal experience is in contrast to mine, my advice is, be true to yourself.

www.ingramcontent.com/pod-product-compliance
Ingram Content Group UK Ltd.
Pitfield, Milton Keynes, MK11 3LW, UK
UKHW041937190726
13854UKWH00004B/1634

9 781847 533746